SEASONAL FRUIT DESSERTS

FROM ORCHARD, FARM, AND MARKET

Also by Deborah Madison

Vegetable Soups from Deborah Madison's Kitchen
Vegetarian Suppers from Deborah Madison's Kitchen
Local Flavors: Cooking and Eating from America's Farmers' Markets
The Greens Cookbook
The Savory Way
Vegetarian Cooking for Everyone
This Can't Be Tofu!

Seasonal Fruit
DESSERTS

~ *From* ~

ORCHARD, FARM, AND MARKET

Deborah Madison

BROADWAY BOOKS
New York

Published in the United States by
Broadway Books, an imprint of
the Crown Publishing Group,
a division of Random House, Inc., New York.
www.broadwaybooks.com

BROADWAY BOOKS and its logo, a letter B
bisected on the diagonal, are trademarks of
Random House, Inc.

Book design by Elizabeth Rendfleisch
Photographs by Laurie Smith
Photographs on pages iv and 146
by Patrick McFarlin

Library of Congress Cataloging-in-Publication
Data
Madison, Deborah.
    Deborah Madison's desserts : from orchard,
farm, and market / by Deborah Madison. —
1st ed.
        p. cm.
        1. Cookery (Fruit) 2. Desserts. I. Title.
    TX811.M23 2009
    641.8'6—dc22

                                    2008046618

ISBN 978-0-7679-1629-5

PRINTED IN CHINA

10 9 8 7 6 5 4 3 2 1

First Edition

For Patrick

contents

ACKNOWLEDGMENTS

As is always the case, a great many people have been involved in the creation of this book, from parents and teachers to farmers and cooks, friends and strangers.

My sweet tooth was first nourished by my mother's baked goods and my father's Concord grape pie. His botanist's appreciation of wild fruits and unusual varieties nurtured my own appreciation of the same long before I made my first dessert. Fruit was always part of our lives, from wild elderberries to secreted pineapple guavas to backyard apricots and front-yard quince.

I would like to think that my affection for sweets was refined by the subtlest of cooks, Lindsey Shere, whom I was so fortunate to work with at Chez Panisse. I am indebted to her love of fruit combined with the sure hand and minimalist sensibility that she so skillfully brings to her desserts.

To those who have shared the fruits they tend with both wisdom and patience, my wholehearted thanks. Among you are Anthony and Carol Boutard of Ayer's Creek Farm; Mike and Dianne Madison of Yolo Bulb; Mr. Ben Laflin of Oasis Date Gardens, tender of unusual stone-fruit varieties; Andy Mariani; peach and raisin producer Mas Masumoto; California almond and walnut growers, Marianne Brenner and Glenn Hoffman; Jake West, whose family has for a century grown the most divine melons; and Mr. Ray Pamperin for cracking the subtle little hickory nut. My appreciation also includes Illinois fruit grower, Theresa Santiago; Larry Butler and Carol Ann Sayle of Boggy Creek Farm; and Colorado stone-fruit farmer, Bill Manning. I am also indebted to grower and seed-saver, Amy Goldman, for all her inspiring books, in particular, *Melons for the Passionate Grower,* which both inspired and made sense out of the sometimes bewildering (though always enchanting) world of melons.

Many individuals are players in the effort to keep good fruit and the preserves made from them alive. Joanne Neft, who helped bring attention to the worthy fruits of Placer County, in particular the Japanese dried persimmon (hoshigaki) and the satsuma mandarin; my sister-in-law, Dianne Madison, who crafts fine and sometimes unusual preserves from the fruit she and my brother grow; and jam makers, Elissa Rubin-Mahon, June Taylor, and Carol Boutard, and Richard Spiegel of Volcano Island Honey, who distill the vibrant essence of fruit into the most divine preserves and honey. And finally, the many people whose names I don't know who also craft the honey, jams, preserves, and nectars from well-grown fruit and who make our lives sweeter for their efforts.

I also extend my heartfelt appreciation to those who have contributed stories, advice, or an idea; that welcomed box of quince, bag of tiny pecans, an exquisite cheese or an exotic Buddha's hand, a box of satsuma mandarins, a bag of hoshigaki. Among you are Greg Patent, Amanda Sweetheardt, Mandy Johnston, Kate Manchester, Karen Stevenson of Wholesome Sugars, Sylvia Byrd, Tami Lax, chef Kim Mueller, Jamie Madison, plus authors Amelia Saltsman, Ken Haedrich, Sylvia Thompson, Geraldine Holt, David Lebovitz, Lucia Watson, Naomi Duguid, and Jeffrey Alford.

As hard as we try, photo shoots don't always coincide perfectly with what's in season, which means there are, invariably, gaps to be filled. I am especially grateful to Robert Schueller of Melissa's Produce in Los Angeles for saving the day with the season's first persimmons and blood oranges, for always sharing some exquisite fruit that has come into his hands, and being available to answer my questions.

To Laurie Smith, my photographer, a thousand thank yous for making my food come alive on the page. It is a rare pleasure to work with someone who is always willing to take yet another photo, who wanders into the kitchen and points her camera into a simmering pot, and who bravely tolerates visitations of wasps and bees as she shoots. Our long sessions together would not have been nearly as productive, or as much fun, without the golden touch of Annie Slockum, who is somehow always a few steps ahead us both. Thank you for making long days seem like short ones, and for helping to make a beautiful book.

Thank you also to Sandy Simon of Trax Gallery (traxgallery.com), who made the white dishes we used that fit so beautifully in the hand and handsomely show off desserts of all kinds. Other potters whose works grace these pages include Doug Casebear, Elisabeth Foote, Vicki Snyder, and David Pinto. For the use of Alex Marshall's beautiful blue dishes, I thank Lisa Falls and Amy Cox.

A book would not get made without people who make books. My thanks to my editor, Jennifer Josephy, at Broadway Books and her many assistants with whom I've worked throughout the duration, especially Annie Chagnot. My thanks also to Peter Gethers and Christina Malach (a giant bow of thanks!) who brought the book through its final moments, and to Elizabeth Rendfleisch and Jean Traina for producing a beautiful book.

A book of recipes, I have found, is most difficult to write when there's no one else in the house to share them with or to issue frank assessments. I am deeply grateful, as always, to my husband, Patrick McFarlin, for being a most supportive companion through this long onslaught of sweets, and his willingness to say when needed, "I don't think that this is one of your better desserts." I could not have done it without you!

And finally, my gratitude to Doe Coover, my trusted agent, who shared my vision and shepherded this book from start to finish.

Deborah Madison
Galisteo, New Mexico

· Introduction ·

If you want to make an apple pie from scratch,
you must first create the universe.
— Carl Sagan

In addition to my long and well-documented romance with garden vegetables, I've had a long-standing love affair with fruit. While I take a great deal of pleasure in cooking with produce, I love making desserts, too. I've been making desserts since I was about twelve, beginning where many young girls do, with crêpes. Years later, at the Zen Center, where my fellow students and I were lusting for sweets, I made countless hotel pans of crisps and cobblers, cakes, and cookies. I made fruit desserts at Greens for the first few years we were open, to supplement the pastries from the Tassajara Bakery, and I've worked on a few occasions in the pastry department of other restaurants. The dessert area is where I got my start cooking at Chez Panisse, working with pastry chef Lindsey Shere, and it's where I spent several years at Café Escalera in Santa Fe, when I realized that I preferred the quiet concentration of confection to the hectic heat of the line.

Despite my affection for fruit desserts and some years spent at their service, I don't consider myself a pastry chef. Rather, I'm a cook who makes desserts. The difference? I think of pastry chefs as having a way in the kitchen that is precise and particular. Pastry chefs' aprons are free from chocolate stains and dribbles of fruit, and they make things that are complex and even architectural. Measurement and exactitude are essential to their craft, while in cooking such things are a bit more relaxed. There's a big difference between sautéing a pear and constructing a pyramidal log of chocolate cake layered with creams and covered with a perfect ganache. (I'm still mildly amazed when I've succeeded in making a beautifully crimped piecrust.) Pastry prefers a more even temper, rather than an impulsive approach.

In general, I favor desserts that don't depend on exacting conditions or considerable manual dexterity to succeed. In fact, the desserts I like most depend not on our skill as pastry chefs as much as on the materials we start with, which is why this collection of fruit desserts is so closely linked to orchards, farm stands, farmers' markets, and backyard gardens—places where you'll find good fruit that will ensure your success. After all, you don't want to go to the trouble of making a peach pie and then discover it has no taste.

"But fruit is so simple!" you might think, and yes, that's true. A tangerine, a peach, a slice of pineapple with a splash of Kirsch, dried figs with roasted almonds or simmered in aged sherry— these are indeed simple with respect to preparation. But to find a piece of fruit that can stand naked and alone on the plate with no sugar, no cream, no crust—that is another matter altogether and one of the areas this book explores.

While I happen to believe that an exquisite piece of fruit is the ideal dessert, I also think there's a place for the crisp with its rough nutty crust, an elegant berry tart, a silky Swedish cream, or that cake that goes particularly well with fruit syrup. This book offers a range of desserts based on delicious varieties of fruits and those foods that flatter them, such as nuts, sugars and jams, eggs and cheeses. These are comfortable recipes to fall into that don't ask you to be an exacting cook— I'm certainly not one! I won't be touting the virtues of making your own puff pastry here (even though I can make puff pastry), and my piecrust is, well, as easy as pie.

ABOUT FRUIT

"Open your mouth and close your eyes; I'll give you something to make you wise."

My husband, Patrick, doesn't enjoy such games, so it was with some reluctance that he went along with this one. I think it's a healthy sign that a person would not willingly be open to ingesting something unseen, so clearly trust is a big part of this exercise. He opened his mouth, closed his eyes, and I popped in a small red fruit. Cautiously, he bit into it. His face relaxed a little. He chewed. Then he smiled.

"What is it?" he asked, his eyes still closed.

"A strawberry," I answered.

"Really? That's a *strawberry*?" he asked. "It's good!"

It *was* a good strawberry. I had found it at a small farmers' market in Southern California, carried it home along with a few quarts of its brothers and sisters on the plane, managing to keep them upright through flight changes and luggage collection. I couldn't wait for Patrick to taste them, for he had always maintained a dislike for strawberries. I thought these might change his mind, and, as you see, they did.

Strawberries want water, and we live in the desert, so we don't have berries except for the few pints one farmer brings to market in June. Arrive a minute too late and you've missed them for the year. What this means is that we don't eat strawberries, since I don't care for the big, hollow-cored, flavorless fruits, also from Southern California, packed in plastic and stacked on produce shelves in grocery stores. These are the fruits that made Patrick think he didn't like strawberries. He had no idea what a strawberry could be—should be. Most Americans probably don't. I've actually seen the strawberry described as a "crisp fruit"—and this in the food section of a newspaper. How far we've fallen not to be able to recognize the true texture, taste, and charm of a strawberry. It's no wonder we have to encourage people to eat fruit!

Over the last sixty years we have completely transformed fruit, making it into a duty food you're supposed to eat because the government and your university health letter say so. So many servings a day—all that lycopene, all those antioxidants, fiber. Yes, it's good for us to eat fruit, but real fruit isn't about its components. Real fruit is dazzling, seductive, and gorgeous. Poets write sonnets and poems about fruit. Artists paint pictures of it. That real strawberry, red throughout—small perhaps, but oh so sweet; an apricot that smells of honeyed nectar; a white peach that caused a young girl I met to turn and say after her first bite, "This is like eating a flower!"—these are some of the charms that real fruit offers. It's amazing stuff, full of aroma, sweet but tinged with just enough acid not to be cloying, exquisitely colored and patterned. Ripe fruit broadcasts its fragrance, announcing to a passing bird or beast that it's ready to be eaten so that a discarded seed or a pit will ensure that its life will be carried on. The lure of fruit should be equally powerful to us human animals. Anything less is like eating shadows.

So where is this good fruit? It could be in your yard if you've got an apricot tree or a row of raspberry canes or a strawberry planter. It could be in a small orchard run by someone who is passionately devoted to heirloom apples, plums, or grapes. And it may well be found at the intersection of local and seasonal foods—the farmers' market—for at least that fruit, for the most part, didn't need to travel far, be picked green, or be limited to the least interesting commercial varieties. It's still possible to experience the kind of diversity that is the sign of a vibrant food culture. The farmers' market is where you'll find the delicate Blenheim apricot with big flavor; summer Transparent apples or the big, chunky Wolf Rivers; the elusive mulberry and the wild huckleberry; even dried fruits you have never seen before, like Friar plums, pluots, and Japanese massaged persimmons.

But a word of caution: Don't assume that everything from the farmers' market or farm stand is stellar. We want it to be, and certainly that's where the best fruit will most likely be found. But there are always those farmers who want to have the first plums or the first apples, so they pick them too green. There are growers who plant nothing but Red Delicious apples over the far more interesting varieties that might be grown, or worse, farmers who have turned to the seriously in-ferior commercial varieties of fruits. There are some who pick everything all at once even if only some of the fruits are ready. A fellow up the road from my house claims to be selling Colorado peaches and Rocky Ford melons from his truck—*in May*—months before either fruit appears. If you don't know the season for Colorado peaches, you're buying fruit that's either eight months old or imported from afar. Let the buyer beware—but better, be an informed buyer. Be watchful, ask for tastes, sniff, ask questions, and be prepared to say, "No, thanks." But we should also be prepared to be happily surprised.

THE IMPORTANCE OF NAMES

My own education has proceeded by occasionally overcoming hesitation, taking tastes, and always asking the names of foods. The naming of fruits (and all foods, for that matter) is tremendously important, yet it's something we don't seem to value as a society, something I find alarming for the future of diversity. If we don't know what something is called, we can't ask for it again. Of course, we can try to describe that peach we ate last year, but names usually work better than hazy

memories and faltering descriptions of color, shape, size, and flavor. Until we can call something by its name, we're like corks bobbing on the ocean, and our world is one of random experiences. When we can name something, that random world starts to assume a shape and contain experiences that can be repeated. It's when we get to know that Arctic Rose nectarine or the plum whose name is Coe's Golden Drop that we can develop an affection for it, look forward to seeing it each year, experience disappointment when there's been a late freeze or devastation when an orchard is bull-dozed to make room for a subdivision. Names create the world, and they engage us in it. Without them, we're lost.

Naming foods is one way to take part in building biodiversity. We understand it with tomatoes, and we can apply it to fruit as well. For each cherry, berry, or grape that exists, there are hundreds of varieties, largely closeted away and soon to be forgotten if they aren't already, especially if their names aren't known. Ask a farmer if he or she would please include the variety's name on the price card. I do every chance I get, and most are pleasantly surprised that you want to know and think it's important. And then they understand its importance, too.

GROWING EXCEPTIONAL FRUIT

Developing fruit varieties involves lengthy trials and often a sustained passion that few of us can imagine undertaking today. Establishing dates and pistachio nuts in this country, for example, took decades of work and a steady vision on the part of a few individuals who had every reason to give up. Fortunately for us, they didn't. The results of such efforts are fruits with names that are definitive, like Desertgold (a yellow peach that can in fact grow where there isn't much chilling weather), and names that point to a place (the Concord grape), a person (the Bing cherry), or a personage (Reine Hortense, a cherry). But when it comes to growing good fruit, all fruits have to bend to certain realities. To better understand the complexities of this world, I asked my brother, Mike Madison, who grows fruit in northern California, what it takes to grow exceptional fruit. His answer hints at just some of the farming practices that go into that fruit you're enjoying for dessert.

CHOOSE THE RIGHT LOCATION
Generally this would be an irrigated desert, which, throughout the world, is where exceptional

fruit comes from. (Think of central Asia, the Middle East, the Mediterranean, California, Chile.) Hot days promote strong growth, cool nights stimulate sugar production, and irrigation is totally under the farmer's control.

CHOOSE THE RIGHT VARIETY

Usually early varieties are dogs. Late varieties also are usually poor. Most late-variety fruits just hang on the tree. They may eventually soften and color up, but they never truly ripen. Avoid types that are described in the catalogs as "especially good for cold storage and long-distance shipping."

FERTILIZE STRATEGICALLY

For good fruit, little or no nitrogen should be applied, but making adjustments in minor elements— iron, zinc, boron, calcium, manganese, and so on—is most useful. Similarly, fertile, deep river-bottom loam may not produce fruit as excellent as a rocky hillside soil. Think of wine grapes.

IRRIGATE SPARINGLY

Plants respond to water stress by making thicker skins on fruit (often a critical source of flavor) and by synthesizing many complex compounds (flavonoids, polyphenols, terpenes) that are the major determinants of flavor, so run the crop on the dry side and make it suffer a bit. Especially in the final week before ripening, the plants should be run dry. This applies to annual fruits (melons) as well as tree fruits.

CARRY A LIGHT CROP

You cannot have exceptional-quality fruit and a huge yield. Part of managing in favor of flavor is pruning the trees or vines to let sunlight penetrate the interior of the plant so that it shines directly on the fruit. Another approach to pruning is thinning the fruit soon after fruits set by picking off excessive immature fruits. For example, you want pears no closer than four inches apart on a branch. The result is fewer fruits but better quality.

If exceptional fruit is going not to a farm stand or to a farmers' market, then it needs a buyer who understands the farmers' undertakings, who is willing to pay a fair price, and who knows how to store and sell fruit in the best possible condition. One such buyer is Bill Fujimoto of Berkeley's Monterey Market. Lisa Brenneis has made a video about Bill Fujimoto called *Eat at Bill's,* a portrait of fruit, farmers, Bill, and his customers who together show what the hands-on approach to fruit has produced. It's inspiring to see what's possible.

However, the hands-on model is not one that fits with long-distance shipping and the supermarket trade. For that, tough, hearty varieties have been developed that can withstand all kinds of abuse and still show a pretty face. Often it's not the fault of the fruit, or the grower, that flavor in supermarket fruit is lackluster, but of the conditions that commodity purchasing demands.

I wish supermarkets were places where everyone could go to buy delicious fruit, but they aren't set up to buy and sell premium fruit. (Co-ops do much better because they often have a strong commitment to buying locally.) In testing recipes, I have given supermarket fruit a fair try so that I can speak from experience. I've learned that if I spend quite a bit of time carefully going through what's there, I can find a few peaches or nectarines that will ripen and end up being fairly tasty. I smell each one, looking for some promise of goodness. I gently press the stem end to see if there's a little give. Most are hard, odorless spheres that have been tumbled on top of one another, which bruises them although you can't see it until they ripen, if they do. If you don't take the time to find those few that have a chance of ripening, you'll end up with fruit that eventually shrivels up. When I made a compote of supermarket fruit, my dinner guest put a slice of apricot in his mouth and then asked what it was.

"But it doesn't taste like anything!" he said.

I don't want this to be your experience or mine—it's too discouraging, too disappointing, and most of all, a waste in the name of frugality.

RETURNING TO THE CHARMS OF LOCAL FOODS

We are a vast country with many climates and microclimates. Our differences and distinctions are something to preserve, protect, and encourage—they are what make our lives and us interesting and diverse. Cherries don't come just from Michigan; apples don't come just from Washington—there are marvelous varieties of every fruit for almost every climate and moment. If we stop looking at the supermarket's seasonless world and explore what our own locale has to offer, it might seem as if there's less to choose from, but what's there will offer delights that fruits imported from far away can't provide. When I compare what my region offers to what I grew up with in California, I can become quite morose. But eating from where I live in New Mexico, I've gotten to know mulberries better, eaten up those big hugs from Jake West, our melon man, along with the unique Jake melon, and enjoyed meeting the couple who bought an old orchard and are bringing back apple varieties that the previous owner ignored. Our apple varieties may be limited, but I've gotten to look for those July Transparents and Wolf Rivers like clockwork. And when I travel, I'm first in line to buy an Empire or a York.

Limits aren't so bad. They shape our lives, give them texture, and pepper them with treats and surprises. The American mode of "everything all the time" flattens out our experiences and makes them less memorable.

BEYOND FRUIT

In addition to fruit, the farmers' market in particular can be a source of other foods to include in your dessert repertoire. There you'll find the nuts of a region—the shagbark hickory nut in Wisconsin; the hazelnut in Washington; the Texas, Missouri, or Mississippi pecans (tiny!); California almonds, walnuts, and pistachio nuts. You will also find oils made from these nuts. One of the best walnut oils (and walnuts to match) I've found was at the Santa Monica farmers' market (La Nogalera), and I've found a lovely fragrant hazelnut oil in the market at Bellingham, Washington, along with three varieties of hazelnuts. Pistachio meal, a residue from making pistachio oil in California, was another interesting product, and there are a good many olive oils being made and sold in California and Oregon markets that would be just fine in the Olive Oil Orange Chiffon Cake on page 236.

In California and Arizona you'll find dates that you'll never find in a store—moist jamlike Medjools, sticky fresh dates, or dry dates to take on a hike. Our nation's farmers' markets are also the source of some truly exceptional jams and preserves made by artisans who work with exquisite fruits. Honey, too, will be regional, reflecting the plants that grow in a particular place. Other sweeteners I've found at farmers' markets include sorghum and molasses (still relatively rare finds), maple syrup, and maple sugar—even sticks of raw sugarcane.

Other unusual finds, but ones that are gradually becoming more common, are grains and freshly milled flours. Popcorn, too! Of course, we can easily buy excellent organic grains and flours of all kinds, but when you bring home freshly ground cornmeal, you might find that the classic

Indian pudding takes on a new life. Good eggs for custards and baking are of course to be found at the market, and also some dairy—occasionally some really exceptional cream, goat's milk, yogurts, and even butter.

One of the most exciting finds at the market today is cheese, for America is experiencing a profound renaissance in cheese making. Many of the best artisan cheese makers can be found at the farmers' market with their fresh ricotta, wheels of aged Cheddar, tangy blues, and logs and pyramids of goat cheese. Whether served alone, with fruit, or alongside some roasted nuts, a fine local cheese makes a superb ending to a meal.

SOME AMERICAN ORIGINALS

Every place has its own unique heritage that comprises foods native to a place or long adapted to one. These are the foods that speak to well-loved flavors and the culinary traditions that surround them.

Discovering such foods in other countries—that unique English apple, the thyme-scented honey of Greece— has long been one of the thrills of travel. We like to bring these foods home with us and make them ours. But in doing so we have often overlooked the unique foods in our own country. Some have been so thoroughly replaced that we scarcely know they exist. The Cavendish banana has long replaced the perfumed pawpaw. Cane sugar has replaced the more delicious maple sugar, sorghum, and other forms of sweeteners. Others aren't quite so endangered but are more ignored, like wild persimmons, which are plentiful in some parts of the country but inconvenient to deal with, or nuts that are plentiful, like the hickory nut, but hard to crack. Yet these foods are so delightful that it's worth keeping your eyes open for them.

In an effort to return to mind and plate those foods that once had value but that are now forgotten or endangered, Slow Food has created a metaphorical Ark of Taste on which these foods can be boarded in hopes that they will be returned to our living foodscape. While Ark foods represent many appealing additions to the American table, it can take some effort to find them. Sometimes just the awareness of their names will do it. You might be in a market, see some pawpaws and Bronx grapes, and think, "Where was I reading about these? I'll give them a try!"

Throughout this book I've named many favorite fruit varieties, not all of which are Ark foods, though many are. Admittedly, you won't easily be able to find Crane melons or Bronx grapes, but

you just might come across them one day. If you do, I encourage you to try them for your own pleasure. It's a case of doing well by doing good, for enjoying such foods keeps them alive in our culture and contributes to biodiversity, rather than hastening its destruction.

AND FINALLY, ABOUT THE DISHES

When photographing soups for *Vegetable Soups from Deborah Madison's Kitchen,* I used a lot of contemporary ceramics. One lidded dish I especially liked was made by potter Sandy Simon, who owns Trax Gallery in Berkeley. Sandy works largely in porcelain, most of it white, and she made many of the dishes you see here specifically for this book. We share similar views of food and pottery, two things that come from the earth.

Sandy writes, "All of the things that go into making food go into making good pots—the hand, the heart, and the five senses. A 'home cooked meal' describes what I want to achieve in my pots. It is a link to what is hearty, loved, comforting, and above all, genuine. Using a good pot is an act of connoisseurship, and sharing a good meal is the culmination of all that went into the making of it."

For me, a good portion of the pleasure of cooking comes from the dishes I use, whether Sandy's white plates and bowls with their subtle bits of wire and baubles, an old Mexican cooking vessel, or a French antique. Often they speak the same language of food, a kind of dialect, if you will, for the impression of hand, heart, and eye lingers in both.

1. BE SOMEWHAT ORGANIZED

Even if you're not so inclined, it really pays to get organized before making dessert. You don't want to see the air go out of your beaten egg whites while you search for the cake pan. Or discover that you're out of baking powder just when you need it! Being methodical is truly worth the effort.

2. PROTECT A PIECRUST

Protect a crust from juice-bearing fruits like plums and peaches by laying down a layer of crushed biscotti, buttered bread crumbs, or nuts finely chopped with a little sugar. The juice will go to these things first, leaving the crust more or less crisp and intact.

3. RESCUE DRY RAISINS, DRY DATES, AND SUGAR

Dates eventually become dry and hard but they can be saved. Put them in a steaming basket over simmering water for about five minutes, or until they feel soft. They'll regain their luster and their plumpness. You can treat dry raisins this way, too.

Sugars, such as muscovado and organic dark sugars, can also become dry and hard. To soften, put the sugar in a bowl and cover with a damp dish towel. Leave on the counter, and after several hours the sugar will have begun to soften.

4. SAVE A FALLEN CAKE

Should your nut torte collapse in the center, perhaps as a result of baking at a high altitude, which is often a challenge, slice off the top and don't worry about the hole in the middle. Spread whipped cream over the cake, then return the top layer. The hole makes a window for the cream and any decorative fruit you might use. Dust with powdered sugar and serve with pride.

Should a cake stick to its pan and present no hope of rescue, tear it into pieces and use it to make a "bread" pudding. When this happened with the Winter Squash Cake with Dates (page 166), it made the best bread pudding ever.

5. TRUST THE CRUST

I was puzzled when a farmer was offering fragrant but suspiciously firm white nectarines at his booth. Could these be any better than the hard fruit I could buy at a supermarket, I asked?

"First of all," he replied, "the sugar spots tell you these are going to be sweet." Sugar spots are those tiny little dots that often appear on stone fruits. "But the real thing you should look for is dull-looking skin. If the nectarine looks shiny, forget it." Then he repeated about twenty times, "Trust the crust"—go by the looks of the skin of the fruit. Dull will be good; shiny won't. Give them two or three days and they will ripen.

6. FREEZE YOUR OWN FRUIT

Growers Anthony and Carol Boutard freeze a lot of berries, and this is what they say to do: "Take your berries home and, without so much as a glance at the fruit, immediately put the carton in the freezer. A day or two later, when the berries are fully frozen, take them out and give them a gentle squeeze while pouring them into an airtight container. They will be perfectly frozen as individual berries. Even delicate, late-season fruit will freeze perfectly." When it comes to freezing chopped fruit, put the slices on a sheet pan, with space between each morsel, and freeze until hard. Then put it in a container and return it to the freezer.

7. PEEL ORANGES AND GRAPEFRUITS PERFECTLY

If you want beautiful slices and sections of citrus fruit, use a sharp knife. Take a narrow slice off the stem and blossom ends. Using a sawing motion with your knife, cut down the orange from top to bottom, slicing away the skin and the white pith that lies just under it. Trim any odd pieces you missed. Now you can slice or section the fruit.

8. WASH FRUIT WITH CARE

Apples, pears, and fruit with skins can be rinsed just before using without damaging them, but soft fruit, like berries, require special handling. Wash them and they'll end up waterlogged and won't be rid of pesticides, which are designed to stick to the fruit in rainy weather. Since blackberries and other cane fruits don't grow on the ground, there's usually no need to wash them. If they're dusty, give them a quick dip in a bowl of water, turn them onto a towel to dry, then use them immediately. Similarly, when rinsing cherries, keep the stems on to keep the water out.

9. READ A RECIPE FIRST

It always pays to read even a simple recipe through before you start. Like a road map, a recipe tells you where you're going and what you can expect before you arrive. Knowing ahead of time can save you the frustration of not having allowed time for a gelatin dessert to set or a tart of minced dried fruits to properly cool. In a hurry or not, this is a good habit to acquire.

10. HAVE FUN AND DON'T WORRY

I promise that these recipes invite you to play and do not forbid you to stray. Hopefully you will learn how interchangeable many ingredients are, what you can do with a leftover dab of frangipane, or that you can improvise a fruit fool or a whip with excess compote. But I hope you will explore the world of fruit and, most of all, enjoy this sweet adventure.

· Ingredients and Techniques ·

Butter: For consistency's sake, I've used unsalted butter throughout the book, but that's not to say that there's anything wrong with salted butter. It's just that the salt amounts need to be reduced if that's the butter you prefer. Given that animal fats are where the residues of pesticides tend to reside, I prefer organic butter, such as that from Straus Family Creamery, despite its higher cost. But then buttery desserts are occasional, not everyday, foods. Cultured butter, made from fermented cream, has a distinctive aroma and flavor. I also love Plugras when I am sautéing fruit in butter or melting butter for any reason as it melts clearly and leaves the fruit clean looking.

Dairy: I vary the kind of milk I use, depending on what I'm making, what's in the house, and who's going to eat. I often use soy milk in places where I know that the flavor of dairy isn't so important. In a custard I'd use 1% or 2% milk (or soy) if it's for me, but I'll use whole milk if it's for company and I want it to be somewhat richer. As for cream, local, organic cream would be my first choice. Otherwise, organic, and always cream that hasn't been ultra-pasteurized. This, to me, is a dead food.

When it comes to yogurt, I am partial to whole-milk—yes, even the yogurt with the cream on top. I think it has a much better flavor than low-fat or nonfat. But while both kefir and buttermilk are low-fat, being cultured products, they have a pleasant tang and a richness that comes from their thickened textures. I sometimes use them in place of yogurt or even sour cream.

With ricotta, I prefer whole-milk but will use reduced-fat. Low-fat cottage cheese seems to be fine. If you prefer vegan "dairy," use it. This is truly a matter of choice.

Eggs: I use organic eggs, when possible, from the farmers' market. Sometimes eggs from the farm vary in size from tiny to gigantic, so I judge by eye to end up with the equivalent of a given number of large eggs. As these are not terribly specific recipes with regard to measurements, this is not a problem.

When making cakes and cookies, room-temperature eggs work best. You can quickly warm them up by covering them with hot water for a few minutes. There are only two dishes in this book with uncooked eggs, as many people are nervous about eggs. It is important to know where they come from and that you can trust their source.

Flour: Here are some of the flours I use.

Organic all-purpose and *whole wheat pastry flour* are the two forms of wheat flour I use most frequently. I like the distinctive flavor of whole wheat pastry flour, but I find I need to balance it with our taste expectations. A crust made with whole wheat flour is delicious with a cottage cheese tart, but it would overwhelm a raspberry tart. On the other hand, taste is always about what we're used to. If that nutty flavor is one you expect to find, by all means use whole wheat pastry flour.

Cake flour is something I use rarely. Being highly refined, it has few redeemable nutritional qualities, but it does make a very light cake. It is the flour to use in the Olive Oil Orange Chiffon Cake (page 236).

Corn flour and *semolina* make standard batters and doughs more interesting. Add a portion of either to a cake, tart dough, or shortbread, and it suddenly has a little more character. Corn flour, finer than cornmeal or polenta, also replaces a portion of wheat flour in many recipes. I find polenta can be too gritty.

The Icebox Cookies on page 34 provide a place to showcase the distinct flavors of particular flours. You may not end up with a classic butter cookie, but you'll end up with a more interesting one.

Bob's Red Mill is an excellent source for all kinds of flours, from all-purpose white flour to spelt and oat and pretty much anything you can imagine. Having had the pleasure of interviewing Bob Moore, I know that he has long been passionate about grains. The high quality of his products reflects that passion.

Gelatin and Agar-Agar: Both of these powders can turn a liquid into a solid. Gelatin is an animal product; agar-agar is made from a sea vegetable. I tend to use gelatin because you get a more delicate, soft set than you do with agar-agar. While I do use agar-agar on occasion, I find that it makes an exceedingly firm jelly that's just a little too bouncy for my taste. But if you are loath to use gelatin and you don't care how firm your "Jell-O" is, try the sea vegetable. The powdered form is easiest to use, and directions are on the package.

Oils: For a neutral oil for lining tins and molds, I use almond oil. Roasted nut oils, however, can be used very effectively in desserts—try a few drops of hazelnut on a sliced Fuyu persimmon, for example, or, if you're making an apple crisp that features walnuts, a few tablespoons of amber-colored walnut oil mixed with butter adds its flavor. Hazelnut oil can flavor a hazelnut frangipane.

Orange-Flower and Rose Waters: These distilled waters are perfumes for fruits. I am especially fond of orange-flower water, but I use it with restraint as it can be overpowering for some people. Orange liqueurs can be used in its place. Somewhat more subtle, rose water is used in desserts that feature members of that family, especially berries. Both are available (and are not very expensive) at Middle Eastern groceries. Look for Cortas brand, which also makes pomegranate molasses, another fruit condiment.

Orange Zest/Tangerine Zest: Orange zest is frequently called for to give a little bounce to a fruit or a pastry shell. However, I find that tangerine zest is stronger and more interesting than orange. If a recipe calls for the zest of an orange, just substitute the zest of a tangerine, even though it's a smaller fruit. Its flavor goes far.

Spices and Herbs: As with vegetable cooking, spices and even savory herbs flatter fruit desserts of all kinds. It's important that they be fresh for maximum flavor. There are many good sources for spices. I am particularly partial to Penzeys. I buy small amounts and replace them often.

Sugars and Other Sweeteners: Sugar has changed. It's organic. It's fair trade. It's diverse. And it has character. It is not, however, raw.

Karen Stevenson from Wholesome Sweeteners explains, "In unrefined, natural, and organic parlance, raw cane sugar is sugar that's ready to eat; but in conventional refining processes, 'raw sugar' is an inedible base material for refined white sugar. In spite of its name, there is nothing raw about crystallized sugar at all; it can't get from cane juice to crystals without heat. While many sugars—Demerara, turbinado, and raw cane sugar—have the same general characteristics, they vary considerably in color and flavor, so, here's to geography!"

Today sugar comes from Brazil, central and southern Mexico, Paraguay, Costa Rica, Malawi, Mauritius, and India. Heavenly Organics and Wholesome Sweeteners are two companies committed to producing organic sugars and sweeteners and to practicing fair-trade policies at the same time. Given sugar's not so distant relationship to slavery, I am glad that we have fair-trade sugar, as well as organic to boot. And while I don't think that organic sugar is better as a food—it's still sugar—I like to think of all the pesticides and poisons that aren't being used in its making and of the fair-trade policies in place.

With so many sweeteners now available, ultimately it's your choice as to which to use. If you especially like a particular sugar, then use it.

White Granulated Sugar: Although I no longer cook with white sugar, I do use it when I want sugar to caramelize. It just seems to work better.

Organic White Cane Sugar (Organic Sugar): It's actually kind of beige, or blond, not white. It has more character, a slightly bigger grain, and adds more than mere sweetness to a dish than granulated white sugar. At the same time, it doesn't overwhelm a dish with its own flavor. It's my everyday sugar.

Organic Brown Sugar: This beautiful tawny (or very dark) moist sugar has a larger grain than standard brown sugar. Both light and dark have a detectable molasses flavor. The dark brown sugar from Wholesome Sweeteners is positively lush.

Rapadura: A powdery brown cane sugar, rapadura is not as refined as other cane sugars, which shows up in its flavor. It gives a warm flavor to custards and puddings, but turns pale foods distinctly beige.

Sucanat: The name comes from the words SUgar CAne NATural. It is, in fact, a whole-cane sugar that retains its full molasses content, which again gives it flavor and character. The small, golden brown grains dissolve quickly when creamed with butter. Sucanat can be used in place of brown sugar.

Turbinado: This light brown crystalline sugar is made by steaming the unrefined raw cane product. Molasses does not figure so prominently as a flavor since only a trace of it remains. The clear crystals are sold as "Sugar in the Raw." Turbinado is crunchy. I sometimes use it to line a cake pan or roll cookie dough in it for that added texture.

Muscovado: Both light and dark muscovado sugars give a warm and distinctive molasses tone to dishes. The darker sugar—and it is very dark and quite amazing—gives a deep butterscotch hit wherever you use it, as in the Butterscotch Pudding (page 188). The lighter is a better choice when you don't want to overwhelm the flavor of an ingredient. I'd use it in any recipe that can take more flavor than that offered by organic white sugar.

Maple Sugar: This is my hands-down favorite sugar. I'm not talking about the tiny jars of coarse crystals but sugar you can find sold in bulk at co-ops in the Midwest, such as Pioneer Co-op in Minnesota, and occasionally at farmers' markets. Unlike the jarred sugar, bulk maple sugar is fine-grained, almost powdery, fragrant, and complex. It doesn't seem to be as sweet as cane sugar, although I use it interchangeably as far as amounts go. It's good wherever brown sugar is called for. I would use it all the time if I could, but since I can't, I tend to use it in rather neutral fare, such as shortbreads or the Swedish Cream with Maple Sugar and Crème Fraîche (page 218), where its distinct flavor will be noticed.

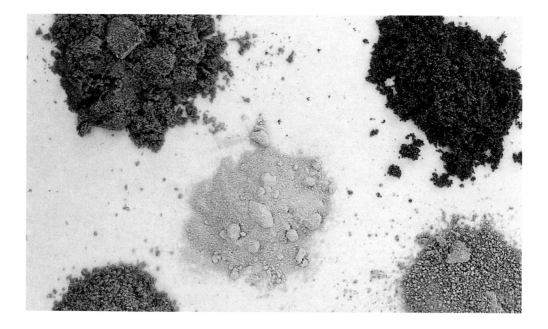

Confectioners' Sugar: I use it for three things: in shortbreads, to sweeten whipped cream because it dissolves quickly, and to dust a cake or tart. A dusting of powdered sugar conceals innumerable flaws and makes something that's perfect even prettier. It is now available in organic form, as is the cornstarch that goes into its making.

Agave Nectar: Because it is a liquid, agave nectar dissolves easily into puddings and custards. Light agave nectar tastes pretty neutral, but I've noticed that it can be cloying if I don't remember to use a half to a third less than sugar. I use it where I want a liquid sweetener that will dissolve into a custard or sauce based on a pureed fruit. The darker agave nectar has more presence, the way brown sugar does over white, but not as pronounced as that. Produced in central Mexico from the agave plant, the nectar's lower glycemic index makes it attractive to dieters and diabetics.

Stevia: The sweeter-than-sugar herb stevia comes in both liquid and grain forms. It has no calories and is intensely sweet, but it can have an odd flavor when used in quantity, so I mostly use it by the drop to correct syrup or a batter that needs a tad more sweetness. I might also use it in a dessert that doesn't depend on sugar for its structure—a custard or a fruit puree—to replace or omit the sugar and its calories.

Honey: I have grown to love honey in compotes, with roasted fruits, and in some pastries for its complex, floral flavor. I use honey where it can shine, whether it's a mild wildflower, lustier thyme or lavender honey, or a really big honey, like chestnut or buckwheat. Honey is one of those foods to look for when you travel. Markets often have honeys that are particular to their area and the plants that grow there. At the top of my list is honey I've found from the Big Island in Hawaii. Volcano Island white ginger honey—well, that's something you just put out with a spoon and call it dessert.

Vanilla: I adore vanilla beans, but they are very, very expensive. While some restaurant pastry chefs make lavish use of them, using whole beans as garnishes and blithely discarding the husks after only one use, I take a more parsimonious approach and use just an inch or two of a bean at a time; then I dry the pod and embed it in sugar. I use it especially where I want to see the minute seeds, in a custard or a cream, and where there aren't too many competing flavors.

· Kitchen Equipment ·

I am not a big collector of equipment. My kitchen is tiny, and I find that a few tools are all that's needed to produce a great many desserts. I do use a food processor for many things, including making doughs, and a sturdy electric mixer, but I also rely on my hands, our most available and sensitive tools. Aside from the usual assortment of bowls, whisks, and measuring cups and spoons, here are those tools that I truly rely on.

POTS AND PANS

Cast-Iron Skillet: A 10-inch skillet is great for baking upside-down cakes—and other cakes for that matter. It conducts heat evenly, and the sugary surface won't burn.

Gratin Dishes, Cazuelas: Whether intended for gratins or something else, I use a variety of shallow earthenware and porcelain dishes for baking not only custards and puddings but also cakes. They look handsome at the table and are much more interesting than glass baking dishes.

Pyrex Pie Plate: A 9-inch, 1½-inch-deep glass pie plate with sloping slides is perfect for making the fold-over pies, which hold more fruit than a tart or a galette.

Sheet Pans (Cookie Sheets with Sides or Jelly Roll Pans): In addition to using them for baking cookies and toasting nuts, I use sheet pans for holding a tart, which provides a far safer means of moving one in and out of an oven than your hands.

Springform Pan: A 9-inch springform pan is what I use for virtually all my cakes. It's just the right size to allow for a good rise and finished height on all the cakes included here. An 8-inch pan makes a somewhat taller cake.

Tart Pan: A 9-inch tart pan with a removable bottom is the tart pan size used most frequently in this book. (It actually measures about 9½ inches.) It provides eight servings, a number that will accommodate most dinner parties or leave you with some, but not too many, leftovers. However, I also like other shapes—squares and rectangles—as well as the larger 10½-inch round.

SMALL TOOLS

Cheese or Nut Grinder: I think this little rotary grater was intended for cheese, but it turns nuts into a feathery flourlike fluff that you want for nut tortes. A food processor simply cannot achieve the same effect. It can cut nuts into very tiny pieces, but the hand grinder actually shaves them. Mine is made by Zyliss, and I've had it for many years.

Cherry Pitter: I have two, a metal one and a cheap plastic one, and it's the latter that has stood me in good stead for years. It takes one cherry at a time, but that's how they work. You've got to get those stones out, or worry that someone will break a tooth!

Custard Cups, Ramekins, Dariole Molds, Timbales, and French Juice or Wine Glasses: I use all of these for puddings, custards, and gelées. Of course, a wine or juice glass would be for a cool pudding rather than a baked custard. Dariole molds, also called *timbales*, are either short and flared or oval. Filled to the brim, they hold about ½ cup and can be used for hot and cold desserts.

Food Mill: This is the greatest tool for separating seeds, stems, and skins from cooked fruits, such as apples when making applesauce. I use it routinely in savory preparations as well, and although I don't pull it out every day, I consider it one of my most important kitchen tools. I usually use it in tandem with a pressure cooker.

Microplane and Citrus Zester: I rely heavily on the Microplane for fine, fine citrus zest that practically melts into a batter. However, when I want visible shreds of citrus zest, say in a syrup or a compote, I use the citrus zester, which removes the zest in long, paper-thin strips, or I remove the zest with a vegetable peeler and then thinly slice it with a sharp knife.

Offset Spatula: The crook in the spatula makes it so easy to spread, say, frangipane over a tart shell without dragging your knuckles through it. Mine is small, and it works in all situations.

Parchment Paper: I use this when I want to prevent a cake from sticking to a pan and flour and butter won't be enough. Unlike wax paper, it has no odor, and pieces that have been used for cookies can be reused.

Paring Knife: A paring knife is the knife you'll use most often when making desserts. I have a number of really inexpensive ones as well as a larger Global knife that can be used for paring and slicing. Of course, you'll occasionally want to use all the other knives you normally do—a serrated knife for bread, a chef's knife for chopping, and so forth. But the paring knife is most essential.

Pastry Brushes: Use them to brush butter onto the top of a galette or brush melted jam over the surface of a tart. Cheap ones are easy to ruin, and you'll replace them often if you bake a lot. Sometimes I turn to paintbrushes, which work well. Best for the purposes of this book are flat (rather than bushy) brushes made of natural hog bristles and about an inch wide or a little wider.

Pastry Cloth (with or without a rolling pin cover): I have found that it really does make rolling pastry easier to use a heavy cotton pastry cloth for your work surface. Just set it on a large cutting board or the counter. Unless you use a cool marble rolling pin (I do and I recommend it), you might want to put the sleeve on your wooden roller as well.

Pear Corer: A little device called a *pear tool* that's used by ceramicists for trimming the feet on pots works perfectly for removing the core, then the stem end, of a pear. The business end of the tool is actually shaped somewhat like a pear.

Pie Weights: These hold dough in place while it's baking prior to being filled. While you can buy aluminum ones, I use dried beans, and I've never had a problem with them, even reusing them as often as I do. And they're certainly inexpensive to replace.

Rubber Spatulas: I now have an array of these in different shapes, sizes, and colors, because I'm always reaching for one to fold in egg whites or scrape the batter out of a bowl. If you haven't done so in a while, treat yourself to one or two new spatulas. They do get old and funky, and it's nice to have those tools you use daily refreshed on occasion.

Scissors: Keep a kitchen pair handy. You'll use them more often than you can imagine, for cutting parchment paper, opening packages, snipping string, and even trimming dough.

Stovetop Espresso Maker: A standard Bialetti Moka Express (at least a 3-cup size—the cups are Italian espresso cups, not measuring cups) lets you brew strong coffee quickly when you need it, whether to drink or to use in a recipe.

Strainers: I use a variety of sizes, from a very tiny fine-mesh strainer to a large one with far coarser mesh. I use them for straining sauces; sifting flour, cocoa, and powdered sugar (just tap on the side with a knife); separating seeds from lemon juice; and myriad other little tasks.

Timer: As intuitive as you might be in the kitchen, a timer really does free you from worry or ruin. It lets you think about other things and then reminds you with its ring that it's time to check on that cake.

Tongs: Tongs are one of the most useful of all tools. While I probably use tongs more in the savory side of my kitchen, I do use them to lift hot custards from a water bath and to pull items off a high shelf on a regular basis. Have several sizes; you'll use them often.

CHAPTER 1

• A Few Basics •

The recipes in this chapter are among the most basic ones that are mentioned and used throughout the book. This is where to go for a recipe for tart dough, a sabayon, or a really good shortbread cookie to serve with fruit desserts. It's also where to go for those really fundamental items like simple syrup, which is used to sweeten dishes when you don't want the undissolved grains of sugar, and softly whipped cream, the finishing touch for so many desserts, from the Sweet Potato–Coconut Pudding (page 185) to a fruit tart to the lofty Olive Oil–Orange Chiffon Cake (page 236).

SOFTLY WHIPPED CREAM

~

I often call for softly whipped cream to finish a dessert, and that's exactly what it is—cream that ends up soft and billowy rather than stiff. Use the best cream you can find, preferably organic. If at all possible, avoid cream that is ultra-pasteurized.

It helps if your cream, whisk, and bowl are well chilled before whipping, although your cream will whip with utensils at room temperature. Warm utensils, however, must be avoided. Cream, like butter, melts with warmth.

Whisk cream gently and stop before it gets too stiff. You're looking for soft, floppy mounds, not rigid peaks. Better to underwhip cream; then, just before using it, give it a final turn with a whisk to get it right. Cream that's too stiff can be softened with the addition of extra cream, stirred in or whipped carefully to the right consistency.

One cup of cream doubles to about 2 cups whipped. You needn't always use a carton—a little goes far to finish a dessert. You might consider using 1 to 2 tablespoons of cream per person and whipping that instead.

Cream needn't be sweetened if your dessert is already very sweet. Often the contrast of unsweetened cream is more pleasing. With fruit desserts that have a tart edge or are not overly sweet to start with, a little sweetening in the cream does wonders. If you care to sweeten cream, do so with powdered sugar, which blends instantly, as do honey and maple syrup. Add it just before the cream is ready. Start with 1 tablespoon for 1 cup cream and taste as you go to decide how much sweetener is right.

FLAVORINGS FOR CREAM

Vanilla (for crème chantilly)

Almond extract

Pureed fruits and fruit preserves

Orange caramel and thick fruit syrups left from poaching

Liquors: Grand Marnier, rum, Kahlúa, brandy, and so forth

Chilled espresso or finely ground or instant espresso

Grated chocolate or cocoa

WHIPPED CRÈME FRAÎCHE AND CREAM

You get that edge of tartness from the crème
fraîche and the lightness of the whipped
cream when you whip the two together.
This can be entirely improvisational, such
as when you want to use up the lingering
tablespoon of crème fraîche and you happen
to be whipping cream, or more intentional.
In the latter case, combine equal amounts of
crème fraîche and whipped cream in a bowl,
whisk until you have soft drifts of cream,
then sweeten to taste with honey and a few
drops of orange-flower water, vanilla, or any
of the flavorings suggested for softly whipped
cream.

VANILLA SUGAR

Vanilla beans are very expensive, and as their
tropical flavor lingers even after they've been
simmered in a syrup or custard, there's no
reason not to reuse them.

Rinse them after they've been used, let
them dry, then bury them in a jar of sugar.
After a few weeks they'll have transferred
their flavor to the sugar.

Use Vanilla Sugar where it will be
noticed—sprinkled over the Cream Cheese
Mousse (page 222). And, of course, it
enhances berries and other fruits as well. As
you use vanilla beans, keep adding them to
your sugar—and don't forget to replenish the
sugar as you use it.

Simple **Syrup** MAKES 1 CUP

IT CAN BE handy to have a small jar of syrup on hand to sweeten drinks, fruits, and purees. The advantage of syrup is that you can taste right away whether your dish is sweet enough, since the sugar is already dissolved. This, of course, is true of other liquid sweeteners, such as honey, maple syrup, agave nectar, and stevia, too.

A classic simple syrup, which is made with equal amounts of sugar and water, is heavy and intensely sweet. A lighter syrup will do the job as well, which is what I suggest. This syrup will be clear and devoid of color and flavor, unless you use organic white sugar, which will give the syrup a brownish cast.

^{1}/2 cup sugar, granulated or organic

Put the sugar in a small saucepan with twice as much water and bring to a boil. Stir a few times to make sure all the sugar is dissolved. You can test this by rubbing a drop of syrup between your fingers; if it's gritty, the sugar has yet to dissolve. If it's smooth, you're done. Turn off the heat and allow the syrup to cool before decanting into a clean jar.

FLAVORED SYRUPS

Tailor a simple syrup to a dish by simmering it with any of the following: vanilla bean, sliced ginger, lemon verbena, lavender, cinnamon, cardamom, cloves, and together or separately, basil and mint.

Maple Sugar Shortbread MAKES ONE 9-INCH ROUND, SERVING 8 TO 10

BEING NOTHING MORE than butter, flour, and sugar, shortbread acts as a canvas for the kind of sugar you use (and flour, for that matter) since they are not competing with any flavoring. For this reason, I love to use my favorite sugar: maple. But, in fact, a shortbread is a good vehicle for testing a sugar you might not know so well, such as Sucanat, muscovado, rapadura, or the Heavenly Organic Himalayan cane sugar (jaggery), which has clear molasses tones but the texture of fine maple sugar. If you want a truly neutral shortbread with no overtones of anything, use confectioners' sugar.

8 tablespoons (1 stick) unsalted butter
$^1/_2$ cup maple sugar plus 1 tablespoon for the top
Scant $^1/_4$ teaspoon salt
1 cup all-purpose flour or whole wheat pastry flour

1. Preheat the oven to 350°F. Have ready a shallow 9-inch pie plate. Cream the butter with the ½ cup maple sugar and the salt in the bowl of an electric mixer until it is perfectly smooth, light, and fluffy. You'll see flecks of sugar, but they will soften and dissolve.

2. On low speed, mix the flour into the butter. Stop the mixer when the dough appears crumbly. Gather it in your hands and press it into the pie plate. It need come only a small way up the sides. Press the tines of a fork around the edges to make a crinkled, fluted design. Bake until pale gold, about 25 minutes. Sprinkle the remaining 1 tablespoon maple sugar over the top. Remove and, while it's still warm, cut into 8 or 10 pieces; then let cool.

USING OTHER SUGARS

Organic sugar: ½ cup
Sucanat: ½ cup
Heavenly Organic Himalayan: ¾ cup
Confectioners' sugar: 1 cup

Pastry for **Pies or Galettes** MAKES ABOUT 20 OUNCES, ENOUGH FOR 1 LARGE (SERVING 10 OR MORE) OR 2 SMALLER (EACH SERVING 6) GALETTES, A DOUBLE-CRUST PIE, OR A FOLD-OVER PIE

I USE BUTTER rather than lard or shortening in my pastry, and while it might not have the brittle flakiness that comes with using those fats, butter does make a delicious-tasting dough.

1½ cups all-purpose flour
½ cup whole wheat pastry flour
½ teaspoon salt
1 tablespoon organic sugar
12 tablespoons (1½ sticks) cold unsalted butter,
    cut into small pieces
1 egg yolk
½ teaspoon vinegar
5 to 6 tablespoons ice water

1. Mix the flours, salt, and sugar together in a bowl. Cut in the butter by hand or use a mixer with the paddle attachment, leaving some chunks the size of uncooked chickpeas. (If using a food processor, pulse until the butter is broken up.)

2. Mix the egg yolk and vinegar with ¼ cup of the ice water. Sprinkle the liquid over the flour mixture by tablespoonfuls and toss until you can bring the dough together with your hands. Add the last one or two tablespoons of water if needed. (If using a food processor, don't take the dough all the way, but stop when it begins to look tacky and starts clumping together.)

3. Divide the dough into 2 pieces if making smaller galettes or leave it in 1 large piece. Wrap in plastic wrap, press the dough into a disk, and refrigerate for at least 30 minutes or longer. Chilled dough is easier to roll out, easier to handle, and absorbs less extra flour, keeping the texture light and

flaky, as it should be. The dough can be made a day or two ahead. Wrapped well, it can be frozen for up to a month.

FORMING A GALETTE

1. Roll the entire piece of dough on a lightly floured counter (or pastry cloth) into a 16-inch irregular circle or oval about $\frac{1}{8}$ inch thick. Fold it into quarters and transfer it to a sheet pan lined with a piece of parchment paper so that the galette can be pulled off easily once baked. When you unfold it, it will be larger than the pan.

2. Add the fruit, leaving a border 2 to 4 inches wide. Trim the dough if you like it smooth looking or leave it ragged. Fold the edges of the dough over the fruit, overlapping them as you go. Depending on how much of an edge you've left, the galette will be partially or completely covered, almost like a double-crust pie. Brush the top with melted butter, cream, or beaten egg white—it will take about a tablespoon—then sprinkle generously with coarse sugar. Bake according to the recipe's instructions.

MAKING A FOLD-OVER PIE

Basically, this is a galette baked in a pie plate. Roll the dough into a circle, then drape it over a pie plate. Fill with fruit, then flop the dough over it, making a kind of double-crust pie but one that's all of a piece.

Tart Dough MAKES ONE 9-INCH TART SHELL

THIS SHORT TART dough, which comes together in a matter of minutes, is the one I use for many of my fruit and nut tarts, altering its flavor with vanilla and almond extracts, grated citrus zest, or different combinations of whole wheat and white flour. While white sugar is neutral and traditional, I prefer using organic dark brown sugar. It adds depth but doesn't leap out at you.

There are two ways to get the dough into the tart pan—patting or rolling—and both are given here. Despite all the words needed to explain how to do this, the making and baking of a tart shell is extremely easy, relying mostly on practice for success.

Wrapped well, the dough can be frozen for up to a month.

1 cup all-purpose flour or $^3/_4$ cup white plus $^1/_4$ cup whole wheat pastry flour

1 tablespoon organic dark or light brown sugar

$^1/_4$ teaspoon salt

1 teaspoon grated orange, lemon, or tangerine zest, when called for

8 tablespoons (1 stick) cold unsalted butter, cut into small chunks

1 tablespoon cold water mixed with $^1/_2$ teaspoon vanilla extract and/or $^1/_4$ teaspoon almond extract

1. Put the flour, sugar, salt, and zest, if using, in a food processor; pulse to combine. Add the butter and pulse until the butter is broken up into pieces the size of baby peas. Drizzle in the water-vanilla mixture and pulse just until large, moist-looking crumbs have formed.

2. Gather the crumbs together into a mass. They should stick together. If there is any dry flour left in the bowl, add a few more drops of water to bring it together as well, then add it to the rest of the dough. Shape the dough into a disk about an inch thick and refrigerate. If rolling the dough, refrigerate for about 30 minutes.

3. If patting the dough into the pan, put it in the center of your pan and then start pressing it out using the heel of your hand. When you get to the edge, begin building the dough up the sides. The walls should be about ¼ inch

thick. It will probably take some going over the dough to get it evenly distributed, but don't worry—it won't toughen. Remove the dough that rises over the rim with your fingers and use it to patch another part of the tart that looks thin. Use a finger to make a slightly shallow impression at the base of the rim so that when the dough slides down during baking, it won't end up too thick at that point. Refrigerate the tart until ready to bake.

If you've chosen to roll the dough, take it out, lightly flour your rolling surface (a pastry cloth is great here), and roll it into a 10-inch round. Ease it into a 9-inch tart pan without stretching it. Fold and then press any excess dough to form the sides about ¼ inch thick.

Partially Baked and Fully Baked Tart Shells

Partially baking your tart shell helps keep the pastry crisp once it's filled. Preheat the oven to 375°F and set the pastry-lined tart pan on a sheet pan. Line the tart shell with foil and fill it with pie weights or dried beans. Bake for 15 to 20 minutes, then carefully pull the foil away from the dough. If the dough sticks, return the shell to the oven for a few more minutes, or until the foil comes away with ease. Once you've removed the foil and the pie weights, return the empty shell to the oven and continue to bake until the crust is clearly set and pale gold, 10 to 15 minutes longer. For a fully prebaked tart shell that will not see the oven again, cook it even longer, another 10 minutes or so, or until golden brown, like a big cookie.

Removing the Sides and Plating a Finished Tart

Set the finished tart on a sturdy jar and allow the rim to fall away. Or hold the base in your hand and let the rim slide down your arm, taking care that it's not too hot or that your arm is covered.

To transfer the tart, still on its metal base, to a cake plate, let one end down with your hands, then use a knife tip to lower the other end to the plate, withdrawing it once it's safely landed. That way you won't accidentally break your tart shell.

Icebox Cookies

IF YOU'RE NOT one to roll out cookies, this is for you. It's for when you want a dry, crunchy bite next to a fruit fool or soft custard. Shape the dough into a log, freeze it, then slice and bake as needed. Or skip the freezing and drop the dough from a spoon. It's easy to double this recipe for a bigger stash.

While this starts out, literally, as plain vanilla, it can be flavored with almond extract or ground cardamom; it can include chocolate or coffee or end up garnished with the perfect half of a butternut or a pecan and dusted with confectioners' sugar. You can also roll the log of dough in crunchy turbinado sugar. Whole wheat pastry flour produces a different but pleasing nutty sort of confection, and, of course, the sugar you use will also influence the taste.

8 tablespoons (1 stick) best-quality unsalted butter
2 tablespoons organic sugar
$1/2$ cup confectioners' sugar, plus some for dusting (if desired)
$1/8$ teaspoon salt
1 teaspoon vanilla extract
1 egg yolk
$1^1/2$ cups all-purpose flour

1. Beat the butter, sugars, and salt in an electric mixer with the paddle attachment until light and fluffy, for several minutes at medium speed. Add the vanilla and egg yolk, beat until smooth, then reduce the speed of the mixer and add the flour ½ cup at a time until all is mixed together. Use your hands to finally bring it together.

2. Tear off a sheet of wax paper about 14 inches long and place the dough on it. Shape it into a log about 10 inches long. Roll it up and then use your hands to pull the dough into a longer cylinder. Leave it round or give it square sides with the aid of a dough scraper. Freeze until firm. (Even a short stay in the freezer will be sufficient.)

3. Preheat the oven to 350°F. Slice the log into rounds about ¼ inch thick or a little thicker and place on an ungreased cookie sheet. Bake until lightly colored on top and slightly darker on the bottom, about 15 minutes. Let cool on the pan. Serve plain or dust with confectioners' sugar.

CARDAMOM COOKIES

You can introduce this spice in two ways: Either add the seeds (known as *decorticated cardamom*) so you can have the startling pleasure of crunching down on them or grind them and use the powder. Better, do both: Add ¾ teaspoon cardamom seeds and ¾ teaspoon ground cardamom when creaming the butter.

ORANGE COOKIES

Using a Microplane, scrape the zest from 1 large orange or 1 tangerine and add it to the butter while creaming. Also add a teaspoon of orange-flower water to the dough with the vanilla. Cardamom *and* orange are a good flavor match (especially with poached pears, quince, and apricots), so you might add orange to your cardamom cookie or vice versa.

CHOCOLATE COOKIES

Add 3 tablespoons unsweetened cocoa powder to the flour for a very dark chocolate cookie.

ESPRESSO COOKIES

Add 1 tablespoon finely ground espresso coffee beans to the flour.

Sabayon MAKES 2½ TO 3 CUPS

DESPITE ITS VIRTUES, which include ease, speed, and sheer deliciousness, a boozy sabayon lightened with whipped cream isn't seen as often as it might be. Of course, its richness precludes frequent use, but a spoonful of this golden froth will set off fresh or poached fruit or a slice of cake like nothing else.

Marsala is the classic wine to use, but really any alcohol can be used, and its particular flavor will be noticed. Some wines to consider are Beaumes de Venise or any other fortified Muscat wine, Sauternes, Champagne, sherry, port, and so on.

4 egg yolks
3 tablespoons organic sugar or honey
½ cup Marsala or other wine
½ cup heavy cream

1. Whisk the egg yolks, sugar, and wine together in a bowl that will sit comfortably over a pot of simmering water without touching the water itself.

2. Set the bowl over the water and whisk until the entire mass is golden and foamy and the thickness of softly whipped cream. This will take only about 4 minutes. While you don't need to whisk frantically, don't stop either, as you don't want the eggs to scramble. Check to make sure all the liquid has cooked and transformed into foam before you remove the bowl from the heat.

3. Scrape the sabayon into a clean, cool bowl and refrigerate until chilled or set it over a bowl of ice if you want to cool it down more quickly.

4. Whip the cream in a separate bowl until it forms soft drifts, then fold it into the cooled sabayon. Keep refrigerated until ready to use.

Almond Frangipane

I HAD FORGOTTEN about frangipane. I don't know why, because it's one of those things you can count on. You can rely on it to be the perfect base for tarts of cherries, apricots, plums, peaches, pears, even pineapple. You could also bake Sautéed Plums (page 84) in individual ramekins of frangipane and be perfectly happy. Plus you can place a dab in the hollow of a peach and bake it.

This makes enough frangipane to give its almond essence to two 9-inch tarts or a free-form galette. Since frangipane keeps in the refrigerator for a week, you can have this ready to go—not a bad idea during stone fruit season. It spreads most easily when brought to room temperature before using.

1½ cups raw almonds
½ cup plus 2 tablespoons organic sugar
¼ teaspoon salt
2 tablespoons all-purpose flour
7 tablespoons unsalted butter
1 egg plus 2 egg yolks
½ teaspoon almond extract
1 to 2 tablespoons Kirsch or amaretto

Grind the almonds, sugar, salt, and flour in a food processor until finely pulverized. Add the butter and process until smooth, then add the remaining ingredients. Refrigerate until ready to use, but return to room temperature before spreading.

HAZELNUT FRANGIPANE

This version uses hazelnuts in place of almonds, and a portion of toasted hazelnut oil in place of some of the butter. It's especially good with pears and excellent with all stone fruits as well.

In place of almonds, grind toasted, skinned hazelnuts with the sugar, salt, and flour in a food processor until finely pulverized. Add 2 tablespoons hazelnut oil in place of the almond extract and 5 tablespoons unsalted butter along with the whole egg and 2 yolks and 1 tablespoon of Frangelico. Process until well blended. Use immediately or refrigerate up to a week and use later.

~

CHAPTER 2

· Fresh Fruit ·

Anyone in search of a healthful and delicious dessert can do no better than to enjoy a good piece of fruit. It asks for nothing—not sugar (well, maybe a little), not cream, neither crusts nor toppings—but only to be picked at its proper time, kept in the right conditions, and eaten at its peak of flavor.

Dessert might be a single Rio Oso Gem peach or Arctic Rose nectarine. It could be a tangle of cherries, an array of melons, or just one luscious variety. And not only fruits, but also those nuts that go well with them.

One of the most memorable desserts I recall was a large white plate that held a sliced fig, some red and golden raspberries, fanned slices of a peach, a cracked walnut or two, a cluster of Golden Muscat grapes, and a wedge of pomegranate. It was a garden of perfect delights.

Whether you offer a single fruit or assemble a platter, gather the fruits from where you live (or are traveling). Consider a grape you've never tasted before, like a Golden Muscat or a Swenson Red. Try to find out the name of that white nectarine that was so good so you can ask for it again. While I've no doubt mentioned fruits that might not be found in your market—I know many of them can't be found in mine—this isn't meant to be difficult or to send you on a shopping expedition, but to spark your own ideas and enable you to recognize some interesting but unfamiliar variety of fruit when you come across it.

Here are a few things to consider when serving fruit for dessert.

1. Start with the best fruit you can find, most likely a local fruit.

2. Fruit generally has more flavor at room temperature than chilled, except for extremely ripe melons and very sweet oranges, which are refreshing when served slightly chilled. (Actually, cellar temperature—cooler than the kitchen but warmer than a refrigerator—is ideal, but few have fruit cellars today.)

3. If you put out whole fruits, provide knives for peeling and slicing. If the fruits are juicy and sticky, have a finger bowl for rinsing off sugary juices. This is not some affected, old-fashioned practice. You'll be doing your guests a favor.

4. As with vegetables, fruits in season at the same time taste good together. This is your most important guide in creating successful plates and platters of fruits. You may be surprised by what fruits are in season concurrently—Fuyu persimmons and raspberries may not leap to mind—but then, such surprises are part of the pleasure.

~

APRICOTS AND FIGS

~

"Apricots or figs? Apricots or figs?"

My friend Charles Shere can't decide which fruit is more exquisite. Thankfully, no one is making us choose. It's apricot season in California, early June during a cool summer, and we have just been to the Healdsburg farmers' market, where we bought a small bag of Blenheims from Combs Ranch in Oroville, in the foothills of the Sierras. The vendor who put them into the paper bag handled them gently, for they were ripe and ready to eat. An hour later Charles, Lindsey Shere, and I are having them for dessert. We gently pull each apricot open and lift out the pits. We hold the halves upright, for a great deal of juice has puddled in the middle of each half. They don't need anything else, but Charles gets up and fetches a bottle of noyaux to the table—vodka long steeped with apricot kernels, whose almond flavor subtly enhances that of the apricot's. It's a perfect match.

Why pit apricots against figs? Because when at their peak, each takes your breath away—and sometimes the power of speech along with it. It's all "mmms" and sighs, and your eyes might even close to better savor these fruits. And also because these are the most fragile, the hardest ones to handle, ship, and store, which means the chances of experiencing them in their full splendor are remote if you don't live close to where they grow. (If you do, buy them every chance you get is my advice.)

While figs won't make puddles of juice, they will make an equally strong impression when you put a few on a plate lined with a fig leaf. Chilling diminishes their charms. They, too, don't need anything to complement them, but they do happen to be good with many other foods—almonds and walnuts, anise-flavored anything (liqueur, seeds, hyssop), goat cheese, blue cheese, mint leaves, raspberries.

FIGS
with Anise Liqueur, Roasted Nuts, and Fresh Cheese

∾

Figs go well with a great many spices, herbs, and fruits. Raspberry, clove, orange, lemon, mint, goat cheese, rose water, and walnuts come immediately to mind. But I think they're especially good with anise—the seeds or an anise liqueur, such as Pernod, anisette, or the Spanish Calanes, which you can drink or sprinkle over the sliced or halved fruit.

Allow several figs per person. If they're fully ripe and tender-skinned, don't bother peeling them. Just rinse them of any dust. Firmer figs should be peeled, the thick white pith removed along with the skin. Halve the figs and arrange them, flesh side up, on a dessert plate and sprinkle some liqueur over them. Add a few fresh-cracked walnuts, roasted almonds, or roasted hazelnuts to the plate, a small mound of delicate ricotta (sheep's milk if you can find it), or a fresh goat cheese paired with an aged one, such as a goat Gouda, for contrast. Enjoy with a glass of the liqueur.

FIGS
with Mascarpone and Pine Nuts

∾

If anise isn't a flavor you care for, and it seems to be a challenging one for many, take this tack instead. Quarter the figs from top to bottom without cutting clear through, press them at the base to open them, then insert a spoonful of mascarpone and cover with a few pine nuts toasted first in a dry skillet until golden, or fresh-cracked walnuts. This would be very enjoyable with a small glass of walnut liqueur (nocino).

BLACKBERRIES
with Rose Water

∽

The floral scent of rose water becomes subtle when added to fruit, yet it underscores the familial connections—blackberries, like most berries, are in the rose family. Not surprisingly, rose geranium leaves have the same effect. Blackberries are delicious by themselves, but you can mix them with black raspberries, red raspberries, or strawberries, too.

Cover a pint of blackberries with 2 tablespoons maple sugar or organic brown sugar and 2 teaspoons rose water. Gently turn them to distribute the sugar, then let stand for 30 minutes or more so that the sugar can go to work pulling out the juices. Serve lightly chilled or at room temperature with sour cream, yogurt, or the Ricotta Mousse on page 223.

AN AROMATIC FRUIT PLATE
of Melons, White Peaches, Raspberries, and Bronx Grapes

∽

This platter of fruit is all about perfume!

While each ripe fruit possesses its own distinctive fragrance, I can't imagine any fruits more heady than ripe melons, white peaches, and late summer raspberries—not to mention Muscat, Bronx, or other aromatic grapes. If you can procure grapes with their leaves, rinse them, lay a leaf or two on each plate, and arrange the fruit on top.

For a half dozen people, choose a ripe melon—such as a Charentais, cantaloupe, Passport, or Gaia. Slice it into wedges, scrape away the seeds, and remove the skin if you like. Slice 3 white peaches around their seams, then twist each one into 2 halves if they're freestones or slice them if they're clings. Break the grapes into small clusters.

Arrange the fruits on individual plates lined with the leaves and scatter raspberries among them.

fresh lychees

THESE DELICATE TROPICAL FRUITS, although still fairly rare, are being seen more frequently than even five years ago, and not only in Chinatowns or Asian markets but at some farmers' markets, too. Their original home is in China and Southeast Asia, but they are grown in other warm, semitropical places around the world, including Florida and now Southern California. Whether you have the red-skinned lychee or the brown-skinned longan, a similar fruit classified in a different genus, it's right beneath their brittle husk that you'll find white, translucent fruit, and within that a smooth seed. Fruit and vegetable authority Elizabeth Schneider says, and I agree, that a peeled lychee looks more like a sea creature than a fruit. It has the flawless, slippery texture of a peeled grape, and one understands why the Chinese call them *longan*, which means "dragon eyes."

Serve fresh lychees well chilled and unpeeled, in a big stemmy pile. Unearthing the fruit from its husk is a pleasing but somewhat sticky task, so you might consider putting bowls of water on the table for people to dip their hands in as they munch their way through a pile of these perfumed fruits.

Canned lychees, by the way, are quite refreshing. A small bowlful makes an instant dessert. Keep a can in the back of the refrigerator so you'll always have something on hand to serve in a pinch. Add the grated zest of a lime to the syrup or a teaspoon of rose water to freshen it.

If you wish to include fresh lychees with other fresh fruit, peel them, then gently push out the seed. Fresh or canned, with syrup, lychees are good with kiwifruit, bananas, pineapple, mangoes, and strawberries.

grapes

BEYOND THE COMMON SEEDLESS green, red, and the occasional black grapes we see in the supermarket, there are some absolutely stellar varieties of grapes to be found, varieties that are unquestionably worthy as a dessert. Some grapes I've tasted rival the sensuality of white peaches. Seeds are often present in our more flavorful varieties, but are a small price to pay for the promise of flavor. On the other hand, there are also some fine seedless varieties such as Himrod and Interlaken that shouldn't be ignored either.

Some excellent grapes to look for are Muscats of all kinds, but especially the Golden Muscat and Black Hamburg, both being highly fragrant and sweet. Lush purple Concords and their paler sibling, the Niagara, are seeded slip-skins with a round foxy flavor that you will easily recognize as that in bottled grape juice. (Both make a great, old-fashioned pie.) Thompson seedless grapes that have been allowed to ripen on the vine until pale gold and translucent are a very worthy grape. And crossing the noble Concord with the Thompson seedless yields the Bronx grape.

Because they're listed on Slow Food's Ark of Taste, I knew to jump at the chance to buy some Bronx grapes when I found a table of them, bunches of them beautifully set out, at the San Francisco Ferry Plaza farmers' market. But before I saw their name, it was their looks that drew me in—the luminous violet flesh splashed with patches of soft rosy pink. Their tightly stretched skins, which make the Bronx grape hard to ship and therefore somewhat rare, offer a teasing crunch when bitten.

Illinois fruit farmer Teresa Santiago points out that in addition to offering fuller flavor, seeded grapes also tend to be meatier and juicier. She favors an old variety called Bluebell ("sweeter than most other Concord-type grapes") and Swenson Red, developed by plant breeder Elmer Swenson.

Price and Canadice are two more varieties—Price are small and compact with dark blue berries; Canadice are light red and larger—that I've seen recently at farmers' markets. Having recently sampled them and Swenson Reds, I can say that all are outstanding.

Grapes are simple to serve. Rinse the bunches gently but well to wash out the debris and dust that tend to cling to the stems, especially toward the center of the bunch, put them on a fruit stand or platter, and either clip off small clusters of the fruits or serve entire bunches with scissors.

LATE SUMMER FRUITS
with Dry-Farmed Almonds

∿

The colors on this platter are purely autumnal—the russet golden brown of the apple, the shiny reddish brown of the date, and the dull wood tones of the almonds enlivened with the splash of orange persimmon and the translucent grapes.

Dry-farmed almonds are harvested from trees that have not been irrigated, which makes them crisp and spare, tasting almost as if they had been roasted. They are more intensely almondy than other almonds. Rusty Hall sells them at the Santa Monica farmers' market, which was the source of all the fruits on this particular platter, but because they are something of a rarity, don't hesitate to put other almonds on a plate in their stead. Late summer or early fall is when the new crop becomes available.

Arrange Golden Russet, Ashmead's Kernel, or another favorite apple, Fuyu persimmons, Niagara or Black Hamburg grapes, and perhaps the first Medjool dates of the season on a platter, including a mound of almonds. Put everything out whole, in clumps and in clusters, with fruit knives so that people can remove slices and wedges of the apples and persimmons.

GRAPEFRUIT
with Pomegranate Molasses

∿

Pomegranate molasses transforms whatever it touches, and it works its magic on grapefruit. I prefer white grapefruit for the contrast in color, but pink is fine, too. What's especially nice is to use a variety of grapefruits, including the large pomelo, just for all the subtle differences in flavor and color.

Allow $1\frac{1}{2}$ grapefruits per person. Slice off the tops and bottoms of each fruit; then, using a sharp knife, cut down the sides, removing the white pith that lies next to the flesh. Next, section the grapefruit over a bowl. If using a pomelo, you will probably have to use your fingers to extract the fleshy segment from the very tough membrane. When done, pour any captured juice into a glass and drink it.

Arrange the segments on dessert plates. Spoon a modest amount—you don't want to drown them—of pomegranate molasses or syrup over the fruit. Garnish with pomegranate seeds and whole or shredded mint leaves.

YELLOW DOLL WATERMELON
with Blackberries

∼

Watermelons aren't only red. There are yellow-fleshed ones, too, heirlooms and hybrids, such as Sugar Lump, Yellow Baby, and Yellow Doll. Who could resist pairing this golden flesh with shiny blackberries and maybe some pink- or red-fleshed watermelon as well? Cut a melon or melons into attractive pieces after flicking out the seeds. Intersperse them with lightly sweetened blackberries in a compote dish. I favor both fruits sprinkled with rose water, with a few rose geranium leaves set in among the chunks and berries. Or puree a cup of any extra melon, squeeze in the juice of a fresh lime, and add a splash of tequila or Cointreau if you like. Spoon this sauce around the fruit. Chill just slightly before serving.

CRANE OR OGEN MELONS
with Sweet Wine

∼

A great many ripe sweet melons take to sweet wines. The speckled-skinned Crane, a California original, is on the Ark of Taste. Melon expert Amy Goldman writes, "The Crane is a rare commodity in a world filled with colorless, odorless, and tasteless melons. It is everything the mass market will not allow. Fragile and short-lived, it is bred to taste good." Ogen, or Ha'ogen, is another fine melon and not quite as hard to find as the Crane.

Either way, cut your melon into bite-sized pieces or scoop out balls of the flesh. Put them in a glass bowl and toss with ½ cup or more of Beaumes de Venise, a sweet wine made from the Muscat grape, or with the Italian dessert wine Vin Santo. Chill slightly and toss again.

Charentais melons and port have long been paired. "They are meant for each other," says Amy Goldman. For an elegant finish to a meal, halve a melon crosswise, remove the seeds, and pour in some ruby port.

CHARENTAIS MELON
with Alpine Strawberries for Two

～

In a perfect world, you might take a very small melon, like a Charentais or Cavaillon, the size for one or two, chill it slightly, halve, and then fill it with tiny tropically perfumed Alpine berries or any roundly flavored, regional berry. Lightly sugar the berries, if needed, and squeeze over just a little fresh lemon juice or Fragoli, an Italian liqueur made from strawberries.

But, given that you probably don't have a wealth of Alpine strawberries, cut each melon into 2 or 3 slices, remove the skins, then overlap them on a plate and cover with the few berries you do have, lightly sugared if need be. Add a few drops of lemon juice or Fragoli and serve.

MUSKMELON
with Sea Salt and Toasted Peppercorns

～

My husband, a southerner, always eats melon with salt and pepper and claims that in fact many people besides those in the South like to temper the sweetness of ripe melons this way. He does this whether it's for breakfast or dessert. At first I thought this habit was a regional oddity, but it makes sense, for a truly ripe melon is so honeyed and intense that it needs that pinch of salt and the warm bite of pepper to bring its lush sweetness into balance. And given that we live in a state dominated by chiles, I would think red pepper flakes would also be good with melon, especially the mild Aleppo pepper.

I rather favor this treatment for orange-fleshed muskmelons (Rocky Ford, Passport, Ha'ogen, and Minnesota Midget), which are the ones we habitually call cantaloupes. But all densely sweet melons are good this way, especially an orange-fleshed honeydew.

Toast some peppercorns in a dry skillet over medium heat until they begin to smell fragrant. Either break them up in a mortar or put them in a peppermill. Present a slice of chilled melon on a plate and scatter on a pinch of fleur de sel and a pinch of the pepper.

melons

EVERYONE HAS A FAVORITE. "Crenshaw!" says one woman, who serves its peachy yellow slices with Medjool dates. "Passport, for sure," drawls a farmer at the St. Paul farmers' market.

"I'd have to say the Charentais," says a third, after giving it a moment's thought.

"Are you kidding?" says his partner. "Definitely a Cavaillon!"

"Aren't they the same?"

Whether we have clear favorites or are confused about what's what, we're often nervous about choosing a good melon. I don't really get the hollow thump technique—all knocks on a melon sound hollow to me—so I trust those farmers who grow mainly melons, because they can actually help a customer who wants a melon for today and another for Wednesday. Jake West, our market's premier melon grower, does just that for his customers, plus he does grow the most heavenly melons, including one named the Jake melon, which has its own story.

In *Melons for the Passionate Gardener*, Amy Goldman brings to light unusual heirlooms and exceptionally delicious melons that you don't often see except at the farmers' market. But when you do find them, it's safe to say that good melons make passionate eaters, for they are one of the most truly sensuous fruits around—including watermelon. Sad to say, melons rarely live up to their considerable potential. Like other fruits picked too soon and then shipped, they are mostly an indifferent lot, low in sugar and with the crisp bite of an unripe fruit rather than succulent, soft flesh. Look for melons that are grown nearby and possess real fragrance.

PERSIMMONS
with Sea Salt, Hazelnuts, and Hazelnut Oil

∿

Fuyu persimmons are the short, squat ones, and, unlike the larger Hachiya types, they needn't be soft to be enjoyed. Slices of smooth persimmon flesh pebbled with a crunchy bit of sea salt and amber droplets of toasted nut oil could be a salad or a dessert. (For a dessert made with dried persimmons, see page 233.)

Because the peels are usually on the tough side, peel the fruit with a sharp knife, taking away as little flesh as possible. Slice the fruit into sections or cut it crosswise into rounds. (Sometimes you'll come across a shiny seed. Just dislodge it if this is the case.) Arrange the slices on a plate; add a tiny bit of sea salt, some chopped toasted hazelnuts, and a few drops of hazelnut oil. Or instead of oil, add a few drops of Frangelico, the hazelnut liqueur.

FUYU PERSIMMONS
with Asian Pears, Figs, and Walnuts

∿

Smooth, crunchy, and crisp—these are the textures of early fall fruits in California's Central Valley. The persimmons and walnuts come in just as the figs are finishing, but there is sometimes a happy moment when all three are available. There's no need to do anything but slice and arrange the fruits, crack the walnuts, and scatter them on a plate in large pieces.

PINEAPPLE GUAVAS (FEIJOAS)

～

My dad knew where all the guava trees grew on the UC Davis campus, their fruits ignored by all but him. Of course he told us kids about them, and we used to just pick them and eat them right there by the bush, they were so good. I always get excited when they come into season in the fall.

Dark green, resembling a small grenade in shape, these 3-inch fruits possess, like the pawpaw, a creamy, beige interior and a divine tropical flavor. They should be ripe—that is, slightly soft and definitely aromatic—when you eat them. Just slice them in half lengthwise and scoop out the flesh with a small spoon. Pineapple guavas are pretty halved and arranged on a plate with other fruits of California's fall season, such as Fuyu persimmons, Barhi dates, the first walnuts, and the first kiwis.

PINEAPPLE
with Passion Fruit

～

The farmers' market in Hilo, Hawaii, has the most gorgeous big golden pineapples I've ever seen or tasted—sugar pineapples. They're sufficiently amazing eaten plain, but scoop a passion fruit over them and you know you're on a tropical island. Pineapples seem to be everywhere today. Not those pineapples, but others that are flavorful and sweet.

Cut a pineapple lengthwise into quarters, or if it's huge, into sixths. Include the crown of leaves if you like or discard it. Cut away most of the core that runs along the top of each quarter, then slide your knife under the skin to loosen the flesh. Cut the flesh into bite-sized pieces, leaving it on the skin, just the way you might do a melon.

Allow half a passion fruit per person. They're wrinkled and awful looking when they're ready to use, but be intrepid. Cut them in half. Inside they're all pulpy and yellow, with round dark seeds, which are pleasant to eat. Spoon the passion fruit pulp over the pineapple.

A RIPE PEAR
with Toasted Five-Spice Pecans

∿

A ripe Bartlett pear may sound common, but it's an excellent pear—buttery and moist, sweet and sensual. Putting fresh pears with these spicy pecans is unexpected. (You could prepare cashews in the same way and use them instead.) Prepare the pecans as described below, let them cool, then coarsely chop. Peel, quarter, and core ripe but still firm Bartlett pears—or another favored variety, such as Moonglow, Colette, or Luscious. Slice and then fan them out on a plate and sprinkle with the pecans.

Toasted Pecans with Five-Spice Powder

Toast a cup of pecan halves at 300°F until they're fragrant, about 20 minutes. Stir them a few times so they color evenly. Heat a tablespoon of oil or butter in an 8-inch skillet over medium-low heat. Add the pecans, sprinkle over a tablespoon of sugar and a pinch or two of salt. Stir and cook until the sugar melts and covers the nuts. Remove them to a bowl and toss with a teaspoon of five-spice power. The nuts will crisp as they cool.

PAWPAWS AU NATUREL

∿

You don't need to do anything to a pawpaw but slice it in half and eat it with a spoon. Or, as some people will tell you, you can just slurp it up while standing under a pawpaw tree. Aficionados say that the fruit should be blotchy and even black on the outside, like an overripe banana, the flesh golden and not white, for this is when the flavor is at its best.

If you have greater ambitions, remove the big seeds, puree the flesh, and turn it into creamy desserts like frozen mousses, Bavarian creams, ice creams, and smoothies. People who have an excess of pawpaws do such things. But a pawpaw is good all by itself.

paw paws

I WAS ASTONISHED when I at last saw—and tasted—my first pawpaw, for I discovered a few clusters of these blotchy gray-green fruits at an Ohio farmers' market only after a long search. Like many Americans, I knew the name from the song "Way Down Yonder in the Pawpaw Patch," but I had no idea that the pawpaw was such an exotic-tasting fruit, much like a cherimoya with its tropical banana-mango flavor and big shiny seeds. Its bananalike notes are probably what account for its other names—prairie banana, Hoosier banana—and other banana appellations for every state where the pawpaw grows. The tropical flavor makes sense, for the pawpaw is, in fact, related to the cherimoya and other tropical fruits. This also explains the similarity in appearance as well as flavor. But the pawpaw is the only member of that genus that doesn't require a tropical climate to thrive.

The clusters of kidney-shaped fruits, which grow on understory shrubs or small trees, were once popular, plentiful, and pretty much free for the taking. But probably because they are fragile and don't ship well (not to mention rather unattractive as fruits go), they never became the commercial success that apples and pears, or bananas for that matter, became. And now that we eat fruit from all over the world, only a few people seem to know about pawpaws. You could be one of them, especially if you live in one of the twenty-six states where they grow. Efforts are being waged to bring back this delicious fruit, however, and a pawpaw festival in Lake Snowden, Ohio, celebrates this fruit's history and its potential. A California farmer, John Lagier, is making them available once again along with Bronx grapes, and I recently bought some from him at a Bay Area farmers' market. Heritage Foods offers five or six different varieties over the Internet in September. Young plants can now be found in commercial nurseries, but while waiting for your own plant to take hold and produce, look for them at (mostly) midwestern farmers' markets. There is even a pawpaw society to further familiarity with this fruit.

FRESH DATES AND
GREEN PISTACHIOS
with Goat Cheese and Fleur de Sel

∾

I wrote about fresh Barhi dates in *Local Flavors,* as one of my most unusual farmers' market finds, and they're so exceptional I include them again.

Fresh, moist dates and green pistachio nuts, which are also moist, enjoy but a two-week season during October, and only in Southern California. However, wherever Middle Eastern markets exist you have a good chance of finding them. Even in Albuquerque I can pretty much count on finding both of these unusual foods each fall, the pistachios invariably a little tired looking, some of the dates separated from their long sticklike branches, but still more than just good.

The stubby golden dates are harvested at their wet, or *rutab* stage, just before they begin to shrivel into the dried morsels we're more familiar with. Once they've gone from their golden-buff color to a luminous

brown, which they'll do several days after you've brought them home, they'll drip with moisture and turn intensely sweet, like a juicy fruit caramel.

The pistachio nuts, which are harvested just before *they* begin to shrivel and dry, are also plump and moist, not yet the crisp bites they'll soon become. They are still encased in their husks, which are soft rather than brittle, and tinted pink and pale green. You peel them away to get to the cream-colored shell, which is also soft and pliable. The tender nut meats within squeak when bitten.

Serve the nuts in a bowl along with a plate of the dates and another of soft goat cheese sprinkled with a pinch of fleur de sel. Take a bite of date, then a bite of the cheese, then peel a few nuts. You can keep this up for a long time over conversation.

FRESH FRUITS (MOSTLY)
with Spirits

Many fruits have corresponding liqueurs derived from the same fruit or its seeds, whose subtle flavors underscore that of the fruit. For example, we have pears and Poire William, cherries and Kirsch, raspberries and framboise, apples and applejack or Calvados. Kirsch and amaretto go with all stone fruits, whose stones carry the fragrance of cherries (sometimes) and almond (always). While not matched in the same way, fortified wines also complement fruits. Splashing fruit, sugared if need be and sliced when appropriate, with a little well-matched alcohol is another way, and a very easy one, of turning fruit into a dessert. (In addition to enhancing the fruit with the liqueur, you might add a scoop of ice cream or serve the embellished fruit with a slice of cake for a more elaborate dessert.)

Here are some suggestions for fruit—mostly fresh, but a few sautéed ones as well.

Apples, sautéed or baked, with Calvados or applejack

Apricots and cherries, fresh or sautéed, with Kirsch, maraschino, or noyaux

Strawberries with Kirsch, Grand Marnier, maraschino, curaçao, limoncello, or strawberry liqueur

Blackberries, raspberries, and other related berries with crème de cassis or Cointreau

Raspberries with framboise

Blueberries with Kirsch (surprisingly!)

Peaches and nectarines with Kirsch or Beaumes de Venise or other Muscat wines; also in chilled red or white wine

Pears with Poire William, late-harvest Rieslings, Muscat wines

Pineapple with Kirsch, maraschino, or rum

Plums with Kirsch, orange Muscat, red wine

Mangoes with Sauternes or rum

Chilled melon with Asti Spumante or Moscato, Champagne, port, or Vin Santo

Bananas with rum, Kirsch, or Grand Marnier and lime juice

Oranges with Grand Marnier, limoncello, or rum

Rhubarb with Grand Marnier or other orange liqueur

CHAPTER 3

· Fresh Fruit in Syrup ·

The desserts in this chapter, like those in the preceding one, present fruit unadorned rather than placed under a crust, turned into a sauce, or otherwise transformed. But here the various kinds are united in syrup flavored with herbs or spices or wine.

A syrup, however light or minimal, gives fruits a jewel-like appearance as well as a sauce. Depending on the fruits you've chosen, their mingled hues may be subtle or bright. Delicate fruits, like berries, are merely submerged in the hot syrup, which heightens their flavors but leaves their texture intact, while those with more durable flesh are simmered until they yield to the tip of a knife. Some fruits are best simply sugared and set aside, leaving the sugar to draw out their juices. Others, like citrus fruit, need only be sliced or sectioned, different varieties mingled in a bowl, their juices barely sweetened.

These desserts are best chilled and presented in a glass bowl to show off their colors and forms. Some are very accepting of cream, yogurt, or ice cream. Additionally, a slice of simple cake, such as the Yeasted Sugar Cake (page 242), or a basic butter cookie (see the Icebox Cookies on page 34) served alongside allows one the pleasure of going back and forth between soft and crisp textures. On the other hand, roles can be reversed and the fruit can take second place, or equal place, to a cake or dairy dessert, accompanying a baked confection or a timbale of Swedish Cream (page 218).

Some fruit requires cooking (like rhubarb) or benefits from it (like apples). A bowl of spice-scented rhubarb, with or without adornment, will make many diners happy, while the same thick puree can be piled onto toast or into a crisp tart shell.

Citrus with Orange Caramel SERVES 4

MAKING FRUIT-BASED CARAMEL sauces is something I learned from Lindsey Shere at Chez Panisse. Because you don't quite recognize it—is it fruit or is it caramel?—it's a beguiling sauce for this dish and others like ice creams, custards, rice or semolina puddings, and Swedish cream (see page 218). As for the citrus, mix and match, using such fruits as blood oranges, tangelos, and Cara Caras, but be sure to include some—or even all—blood oranges for their lush color and berrylike flavor. Blood orange juice, even just a little, deepens the sauce to a burnished red.

Having your knife razor-sharp makes peeling oranges a snap.

8 citrus fruits for the compote (see headnote)
$1/3$ cup organic sugar
$1/2$ cup fresh orange juice, preferably blood orange
1 short cinnamon stick
1 clove
A few drops orange-flower water
Pomegranate seeds and/or fresh mint sprigs for garnish

1. Remove a wide band of the zest from 1 orange and slice into thin strips. Boil for 1 minute, then drain and set aside. Peel the rest of the fruits (see page 13), cut them into rounds, and put them in a bowl.

2. Melt the sugar over medium heat in a light-colored skillet, stirring often until it turns a rich but not too dark caramel color. Standing back from the pan, pour in the juice. It will bubble ferociously, and the caramel will clench into a knot, but don't worry. Add the reserved orange zest, cinnamon stick, and clove. Continue cooking and after about 5 minutes the caramel will have dissolved.

3. Add the orange-flower water, slide in the fruits and swish them around, then pour the fruits and sauce into a bowl. Serve chilled or at room temperature, garnished with a handful of pomegranate seeds and/or sprigs of mint.

Winter Jewel Compote with Pomegranate Seeds SERVES 6

ONE CANNOT GO wrong with the jewel-like colors and clean, bright flavors of winter citrus, but citrus fruits can be a little tedious to prepare, at least for a crowd. For a small group, though, they're no problem and make a light, bright finish to a winter meal.

There is no one magical combination of fruits, so what's given here is a suggestion. You may need to replace Cara Cara oranges or a pomelo with other fruits. The pomelos are those enormous grapefruitlike citrus that make an appearance around the Chinese New Year. Under a great deal of spongy pith lie pale, large segments that are more subtle than most citrus. Cara Caras are oranges whose flesh is closer to salmon pink than orange. Fun for the color, but use another kind of orange if you can't find them.

2 red-fleshed grapefruits
3 Cara Cara or navel oranges
4 blood oranges
4 tangerines, depending on size
1 pomelo, if available
1 small pomegranate
Light aromatic honey, such as orange blossom
Mint leaves

1. Peel all the citrus fruits save 1 blood orange with a sharp knife (see page 13). Juice the fourth blood orange into a small bowl. Slowly, so that it won't splatter, cut the pomegranate into quarters, then, working over a bowl, dislodge the seeds from the clinging membrane with your fingers. Leaving some seeds attached to the skin, squeeze out the juice and add it to the blood orange juice.

2. Either section the peeled citrus or slice crosswise, as you wish. Arrange them attractively on dessert plates.

3. Stir the honey into the blood orange and pomegranate juice to taste, then drizzle it over the fruit. Garnish with mint leaves and serve.

Seckel Pears Poached

in Red Wine with Pepper and Star Anise SERVES 6

SHORT AND SQUAT with dull green skin, Seckel pears look unpromising. But once that hidelike skin has been sliced away, they are juicy and aromatic with hints of citrus. They're stunning poached whole—and certainly easiest to handle that way—but their small size yields only a few bites. (For this reason, you might prefer a larger pear, halved, peeled, and cored.) Serve them, the red wine first reduced to a syrup, with a knife and spoon so that the flesh can be sliced away from the core. Because they're so small, you might feature them as part of a compote that includes poached dried fruits (page 144), alongside a serving of Honeyed Semolina Pudding (page 180), or with a fresh, slightly tangy goat cheese.

2 cups red wine
1/2 cup honey or organic sugar
1 star anise
1 short cinnamon stick
1/2 teaspoon peppercorns, toasted in a dry skillet until fragrant
1 large, thin piece lemon or orange peel
12 whole Seckel or Forelle pears or 4 small Boscs, halved and cored

1. Bring the wine and honey to a boil with the spices and citrus peel in a 2-quart saucepan. Meanwhile, slice off the tough skins of the pears with a paring knife in neat strokes and add each pear to the pan. Cover and simmer for 30 minutes, or until tender when pierced with a knife. Then turn off the heat and set aside to cool. Transfer the pears to a serving dish and return the sauce to the stove.

2. Bring the liquid to a boil and reduce until tiny bubbles cover most of the surface and the wine has a syrupy consistency, 5 to 10 minutes. Pour this over the fruit or use it as a sauce to spoon over the fruit once it's served.

Mangoes with **Minced Strawberries** SERVES 2

You don't always have to have pounds of fruit to make a fruit dessert. This compote uses a handful of strawberries, about what a small garden would offer at any one time, and one large (or two small) mangoes. It's pretty, simple, and sufficient. I love mincing a few choice strawberries to spoon over ice cream or another fruit. It's unexpected and a good way to share a small treasure.

This is excellent with the Coconut Rice Pudding Cake (page 182).

A small handful of ripe, fragrant strawberries
1 teaspoon organic sugar
Juice of 1 key lime
2 yellow kidney-shaped Ataulfo mangoes or 1 larger variety (see A Seasonal Note)

1. Rinse the berries, set them on a clean towel to wick up the moisture, then remove the leaves. Dice them into small pieces. Put them in a bowl and toss with the sugar and lime juice. As they stand, they'll release their juices to make a little sauce.

2. Peel the mangoes. Then, using a sharp knife, slice them into neat pieces. They won't be at all uniform because of the big seed that runs down the center of the fruit. Divide between 2 plates, then spoon the strawberries and their juice over and around the mango.

A Seasonal Note

Mangoes and strawberries overlap in Southern California farmers' markets as well as in supermarkets. Champagne, or Ataulfo mangoes, the small yellow ones, appear in May, the big green-skinned silky-fleshed Keitt in late summer, and in between are Hayden, Tommy Atkins, and others. Strawberries are not just for June but span the months from late spring through fall.

Strawberries in **Red Wine Syrup** SERVES 2 OR 3

THE WINE TURNS these berries an electric shade of red, at least for six hours or so, after which they lose that luster but remain good to eat. They're lovely served with sections of orange as well as plain. Even though I suggest a lighter wine, pretty much whatever wine you choose will become even-tempered by the time the strawberries yield their juice.

1 cup red wine, such as Beaujolais, Valpolicella, or Pinot Noir
$1/3$ to $1/2$ cup organic sugar
$1/8$ teaspoon toasted peppercorns, lightly crushed
1 heaping pint basket of ripe strawberries (about $2^1/2$ cups)

1. Put the wine, sugar, and peppercorns in a small saucepan and bring to a boil. Simmer just until small bubbles form around the edges of the pan, but don't let them cover the entire surface or the syrup will be too thick. This should take 15 minutes.

2. While the wine is reducing, rinse the berries and set them on a clean dishtowel to wick up the moisture. If they're large, slice them into quarters or eighths; smaller berries can be sliced in half. When the syrup is cooked, pour it through a strainer over the fruit. Cover and let stand for at least an hour so that the strawberries yield their juices. Give them an occasional turn with a soft spatula so that all the berries come in contact with the wine, then divide the berries among small glasses— preferably the little bar glasses from France or Italy—and pour the syrup over them. Serve chilled with orange sections or a spoonful of cream if desired.

Pineapple and Kiwi with **Basil Syrup** SERVES 6

BASIL AND PINEAPPLE? It's a great combination. I've used purple basil, Thai, Piccolo Fino, and Genovese, and they're all good, but I'm particularly drawn to the cinnamon-scented Thai basil for its floral spicy tones and the purple basil for its color. Be sure to set aside a few small leaves or flowers for garnish.

A ripe kiwi is not the tart, sour fruit many people encounter (and dislike), but a luscious tropical wonder. Sadly, it suffers the same demands of shipping and storing that tomatoes and figs endure, which makes it hard to find truly ripe kiwi outside of a farmers' market. However, I have on more than one occasion surprised myself by forgetting about a bowl of kiwifruits, then finding them soft and utterly melodious in the mouth—the way they should be.

3 to 4 tablespoons organic sugar
Grated zest and juice of 2 limes
1 pineapple (about 3 pounds)
3 kiwifruits, yellow, green, or both
2 tablespoons Kirsch or rum (optional)
Approximately 2 tablespoons slivered basil leaves
Basil leaves and/or basil flowers for garnish

1. Bring 3/4 cup water to a boil with the sugar. Simmer until the sugar is completely dissolved, after a few minutes. Add the lime zest and steep while you prepare the pineapple.

2. Cut off the top of the pineapple. Then using a very sharp knife, slice down the sides, removing the eyes as you go. Quarter the fruit lengthwise, cut away the core, then slice into fan-shaped pieces about 3/8 inch thick. Peel then slice the kiwi into rounds and intersperse them among the pineapple slices. Squeeze on the lime juice and add the Kirsch, if using.

3. Add the slivered basil to the syrup and immediately pour it over the fruit. Chill and then serve, garnished with additional basil leaves or their flowers.

Small Melons Filled with Summer Fruits, Herbs, and Wine

SERVES 4

Filling melons with fruit is hardly a new idea. But filling a halved Charentais, Minnesota Midget, or other small melon with a mixture of fruits, sweet herbs, and sparkling wine brings this dessert to quite another level. Measurements won't be—can't be—exact. Improvise with what you have.

Lacking a small melon, use any fully ripe variety, fill it with fruit, and serve from the melon. Make this as full and elaborate as your supply of herbs, flowers, and fruit allows or keep your melon and fruit on the austere side, adding but a single fruit and a sprig of mint if that's all you have.

2 Charentais or other small, perfumed melons

3 cups mixed fruit, such as raspberries, strawberries, stemmed huckleberries, and sprigs of currants

Simple syrup or agave nectar

A small handful of aromatic, edible herbs and/or flowers, such as lemon verbena leaves, small sprigs of lemon thyme, lavender blossoms separated from their spikes, and small mint leaves

1/2 cup Beaumes de Venise, Moscato di Asti, or port

Edible blossoms for garnish

1. Rinse the melons of any surface dirt and cut them in half. Make sure they can stand firmly. If they wobble, slice a little off each base to stabilize them.

2. Scoop out the seeds and discard them, then carefully remove some of the flesh using a spoon or small melon scoop. Put the melon flesh in a bowl, add the mixed fruit, then sweeten with syrup to taste. Fold in the herbs and/or flowers and pour over the wine. Spoon this fruit salad into the melons and refrigerate for an hour.

3. Serve the fruit-filled melons topped with something edible and fetching—a nasturtium flower, a spray of jasmine, a rose petal, or a few sprigs of mint or lavender.

White Peaches in Lemon Verbena and Lavender Syrup SERVES 6

LEMON VERBENA DOESN'T grow with much enthusiasm in New Mexico, so I was delighted to discover that dried leaves, when thrown into bubbling syrup, expand, turn bright green, and infuse it with their flavor. They should be fairly freshly dried, though; if yours are a few years old, don't bother. Lavender keeps its potency better when dried, but in both cases, use fresh if at all possible.

This is a simple, single-fruit dessert to which you could easily add a basket of small strawberries or raspberries. Serve with Almond–Corn Flour Cake (page 239) or Olive Oil–Orange Chiffon Cake (page 236).

3 to 4 tablespoons organic sugar
A small handful of fresh lemon verbena leaves or 12 dried
3 spikes of culinary (Provençal) lavender or $1/4$ teaspoon dried
6 large white peaches or nectarines

1. Combine the sugar, lemon verbena, and lavender in a small saucepan with 1 cup water and bring to a boil. Stir to dissolve the sugar, lower the heat, and simmer for 4 minutes. Turn off the heat and steep for at least 15 minutes.

2. Dip the peaches into a pot of boiling water for 5 seconds, then remove them to a bowl of cool water to stop the cooking. Slip off the skins.

3. Slice the peaches into halves or quarters directly into a glass bowl, then pour the syrup over them through a strainer. Put a few of the lemon verbena leaves and lavender flowers back in with the peaches. Lay a piece of parchment paper or wax paper directly over the fruit and refrigerate. Serve within an hour or two.

Red Berry Soup with **White Peaches and Summer Berries**

SERVES 4 TO 6

PEACHES (OR NECTARINES),
raspberries, red currants,
strawberries, and other berries
that share the season are happy
companions. And this is the
place to use small amounts
of garden treasure, such as a
handful of fraises des bois, a
perfect little strawberry, or
a sprig of golden currants.

While the fruit will be plenty
for some, others might want a
bit more in the bowl. It could
be a scoop of ice cream, Greek
yogurt, ricotta cheese, or mousse.

THE SOUP

2½ cups red raspberries or mixed raspberries, red currants,
   and strawberries (see Note)
2 tablespoons organic sugar
Few drops lemon juice or 1 teaspoon rose water

THE FRUIT

3 or 4 peaches or nectarines, white and/or yellow fleshed
1 scant cup mixed berries, such as golden raspberries,
   blackberries, and currants
2 rose geranium leaves with their blossoms, lavender sprigs,
   or sprays of currants for garnish

1. To make the soup, put the berries in a small pan with the sugar and ½ cup water. Bring to a boil, then simmer for about 1½ minutes, breaking up the fruit with a masher or pestle. Turn off the heat, let stand for 5 minutes, and then pour into a sieve. Using a rubber scraper, force out as much juice as possible. You should have about 1¼ cups. Let cool, then stir in the lemon juice or rose water, adding more to taste if desired. Cover and refrigerate.

2. For the fruit, dip the peaches into a pot of boiling water for 5 seconds, then remove them to a bowl of ice water to stop the cooking. Slip off the skins. (Or refrigerate the fruit with the skins intact until needed.) *(continued)*

3. To serve, set out shallow bowls and divide the soup among them. Slice the peeled peaches and divide them among the bowls. Scatter the berries among the sliced fruits, saving any extra-special fruits, such as a spray of currants or fraises des bois, for the crowning touch. Add a scoop of yogurt, ice cream, or other embellishment if desired, then top with the rose geranium leaves and their blossoms, lavender sprigs (with some of the individual blossoms removed and scattered over the fruit), or sprays of currants.

NOTE
If you don't have access to fresh local raspberries, make the fruit soup using frozen ones (see page 260).

rhubarb

THOSE WHO HAVE RHUBARB in their gardens no doubt find its appearance a welcome if somewhat startling sign of spring. It emerges as a fistlike ball pushing through the earth, and you can't imagine that leaves will eventually unfold from such knotty material, but they do. They start out yellow and become greener and larger as the stalks lengthen. And, although we think of rhubarb as red, in fact it can be either red or green. Victoria, for example, is an heirloom that produces mostly green stalks and only the occasional red one. Cooked, the green stalks break down into a subtle pea-green puree but taste just like the red varieties.

Technically, rhubarb is a vegetable, even though we habitually refer to it as a fruit. At one point, the U.S. Customs Court arrogantly ruled that rhubarb was a fruit, as if government can overrule the laws of botany! And that's pretty much how we think about rhubarb, as long as there's plenty of sugar. Without a sweetener, rhubarb is *sour*. Add to that the fact that the leaves are poisonous, and you might wonder how humans came to even consider eating such a plant. But after a long winter diet of meat and starch, you might be able to imagine that rhubarb would be welcome—not as pie but as a tonic to get one's sluggish system going again. Before sugar was plentiful and cheap, rhubarb was cooked in soups and sauces, especially in the chilly northern parts of the world.

When it comes to dessert, however, rhubarb figures well in compotes and fools, tarts, crisps, and compotes. Regardless of how it's cooked, rhubarb nearly always falls apart into a puree, with the exception of the Baked Rhubarb on page 80.

Rhubarb is flattered by a constellation of other fruits and flavors. Orange is a constant whether it's the fruit, zest, orange-flower water, or liqueur. Blood oranges are even better, given their crimson color and more complex flavor, but grapefruit and Meyer lemon are interesting as well. I always like clove with rhubarb as well as the orange, and I turn to that duo over and over. But spices like cinnamon, cardamom, nutmeg, vanilla, and ginger flatter as well. Maple syrup and maple sugar are good alternatives to white sugar, having more depth of flavor.

Strawberries are endlessly paired with rhubarb, but that's mostly because we think of them as seasonally compatible—the first fruits. And they do make a great pair. But since rhubarb thrives where weather is cool and can therefore persist well into summer, there are other options. One July I bought long, handsome stalks of rhubarb from a farm in Washington just when the blackberries were in season, and the two made a stellar compote.

Late Summer Rhubarb and **Blackberry Compote**

SERVES 6

BLACKBERRIES ARE JUST as appealing as strawberries with rhubarb, if not more so, and certainly far more dramatic looking. But since strawberries are often around then, too, why not have some of both here?

Use the poaching liquid to make Rhubarb Syrup: Pour the juice off the cooked fruit and boil it until thick and syrupy, a matter of 15 minutes or fewer. Add a teaspoon or two of orange-flower water or orange liqueur to taste. Cool, then refrigerate. Use this syrup to embellish a Rhubarb Fool (page 209) or the Individual Rhubarb Tarts (page 124).

$1^1/2$ pounds rhubarb (about 4 cups cut up)
Juice of 1 orange plus 3 wide strips of zest
$3/4$ cup organic sugar or $1/2$ cup agave nectar
One 1-inch piece vanilla bean, slit lengthwise
1 to 2 cups blackberries
$1^1/2$ teaspoons rose or orange-flower water, or more to taste

1. Rinse the rhubarb, trim the stalks, then cut them into pieces 1 inch long. Measure the orange juice and add enough water to make 2 cups. Put it in a wide pan with the orange zest, sugar, and vanilla bean. Bring to a boil, stir to dissolve the sugar, then reduce the heat to a quiet simmer. Add the rhubarb and cook carefully, turning the pieces so that they cook evenly. Often a piece that is cooked on one side is still a bit firm on the other side. It takes only about 10 minutes for them to be done.

2. Use a slotted spoon to remove each piece as it finishes cooking to a wide bowl, alternating with the blackberries.

3. Return the poaching liquid to the stove and boil until only ¾ cup remains, after 8 to 10 minutes. Stir in the rose water, then pour the syrup over the fruit. Refrigerate and serve cold.

CHAPTER 4

· Roasted and Sautéed Fruit ·

Heat brings out the flavors of fruits, while high heat, produced during roasting and sautéing, brings out fruits' sugars. The result is a slick of caramel on the base of a skillet or baking dish, which, when diluted with a little water, alcohol, or cream, adds a hint of burnt sugar. While this isn't the main reason for roasting and sautéing fruits, these methods can improve fruits whose flavors lack luster. And when fruits are at the peak of their flavor, such cooking concentrates their sugars and flavors so that a roasted ripe fig or sautéed pear can possess such intensity that only a few bites are needed to satisfy. Quince, which I've happily poached for years, emerges from the oven with far more character. Of course, creamy accompaniments, from cream to ice cream, are especially compatible with such warm, concentrated fruits.

Many fruits can be treated to a turn in the oven or the skillet—bananas and pineapples, pears and apples, figs and peaches. I tend to prefer high-heat cooking in the cooler months, when the warmth of the oven is appreciated. Even though there is something of a fad for roasting and grilling summer fruits, I am loath to be inside near a hot oven on a warm summer's night while everyone else is outdoors or to return to the grill to cook those peaches once dinner is done. Still, there are those evenings when an afternoon rain has cooled everything off and it's rather a nice change to bake a peach or sauté an early season pear. And if you're using the oven in any case, adding a dish of plums dusted with orange sugar makes perfect sense.

Plump Golden Apples SERVES 4

IN ABOUT 15 minutes you can have a pan of plump, golden wedges of fruit that resemble fried potatoes, only they melt in the mouth—and they're apples! It was a recipe in *Lulu's Provençal Table* that got me out of my sautéed apple rut and onto this approach. While Lulu specifies Reinettes, they're hard to find here. Gala apples do hold their shape, as do Jonathans, but even apples that want to get puffy will work. I've used July Transparent, a tart summer apple that after about 10 minutes looks as if it might explode. It doesn't, though, and this treatment sweetens these tart fruits right up.

4 large apples
2 tablespoons unsalted butter
1 to 1½ tablespoons organic sugar
¼ cup applejack, Calvados, whiskey, or sherry
One 1-inch piece cinnamon stick or a 2-inch piece vanilla bean, halved lengthwise

1. Remove the cores with an apple corer, then cut the apples into quarters or sixths. Slice the skin off each piece.

2. Choose a 10-inch pan with a tight-fitting lid that will hold the apples in a single layer. Melt the butter over medium heat, then add the apples and sprinkle on the sugar, using the larger amount if they're tart. Raise the heat, shuffle the pan back and forth to mix the apples evenly with the butter and sugar, then add the applejack and cinnamon. Reduce the heat to low, cover the pan, and cook for 15 minutes. Check to see if the apples are tender by piercing them with a knife. If not, cook for a few minutes longer, or until tender.

3. Remove the lid, raise the heat a little, and continue cooking, reducing the liquid as you do so, until the apples are golden, after several minutes. Serve warm.

Warm Apricots with Honey and Yogurt

If your fresh apricots aren't already dripping with honeyed nectar, this simple turn in the oven will set things right. I've even forced an indifferent commercial variety into tasting pretty good by using this method. Some finely chopped pistachio nuts and a few purple bits of lavender blossom scattered over this fruit can look festive and taste exotic. Otherwise just enjoy these plain and sprinkle a tiny bit of cardamom or cinnamon over the yogurt.

$1^1/2$ apricots per person, or more if they're very small
Honey or maple syrup
Yogurt, crème fraîche, or mascarpone
Finely chopped pistachio nuts
A few pinches of aromatic lavender blossoms

Preheat the broiler. Cut the apricots in half along their seams and remove the pits. Set them, cut side up, in a shallow gratin dish. Spoon honey into each cavity, then broil until bubbly, about 5 minutes. Serve with a spoonful of cold creamy yogurt over each half, followed by the chopped pistachios and lavender blossoms.

USING A TOASTER OVEN

This is a good dessert for just one or two people, but you might not want to heat the whole oven for so few. If you have a toaster oven, put the apricots in a small dish and bake them at 375°F until they're soft and the honey is bubbling, 12 to 15 minutes.

WARM PLUOTS OR APRIUMS WITH HONEY AND YOGURT

If you're a fan of these hybrid fruits, a plum-apricot cross, use them the same way as the apricots, but be prepared to cook them a little longer if they are very firm.

Hazelnut-Stuffed Peaches, Pears, or Apricots

SERVES 4

ROASTED HAZELNUTS, GROUND with brown sugar, hazelnut oil, and butter, fill the cavities of plump peaches, pears, and other fruits. The filling keeps for weeks in the refrigerator or freezer, the makings for a last-minute dessert.

Incidentally, a toaster oven can be very efficient both for toasting nuts and for baking fruit. It's a simple matter to stuff a few apricots and slide them into a toaster oven (350°F for about 10 minutes). Just like that, you have dessert for you and one other.

When it comes to peaches, leave the skins on, as they act as a container for the flesh and make them easy to handle. Look for freestone varieties—Elberta, Flavorcrest, or Suncrest.

$3/4$ cup toasted hazelnuts
5 tablespoons maple sugar or organic brown sugar, plus extra for the top
$1/8$ teaspoon salt
$1^{1}/2$ tablespoons hazelnut oil
$1^{1}/2$ tablespoons unsalted butter
4 freestone peaches, ripe but still firm
Frangelico, sweet wine, or water

1. Grind the nuts with the sugar and salt in a food processor until small but gritty pieces remain. Add the oil and butter and pulse until the mixture is moist and almost sticky.

2. Wipe the peaches with a damp cloth, then slice them around their seams (the indentation in the skin), going clear to the pit. Twist the halves apart and remove the stones. Enlarge the cavity a bit with a teaspoon.

3. Mound the hazelnut mixture into the fruits, then put them in a baking dish. Pour in a little Frangelico and bake until the filling is lightly browned and the fruits are soft, about 25 minutes. The peaches will give off their juices, which mingle with the Frangelico and butter to make a sauce. Serve while they're still warm, but not piping hot.

Two Rhubarb Purees

One puree is delicate, seasoned only with citrus, while the other more robust, bursting with cinnamon, clove, and maple sugar. Serve each of them cold with a bit of cream poured on top. Turn them into Rhubarb Fools (page 209), or use the mixture to fill a tart shell. If an excess of juice is produced, reduce it and use it as a glaze or to enhance the flavor and sweetness of the rhubarb.

Green Rhubarb Puree with Grapefruit

MAKES 2 1/2 TO 3 CUPS

2 1/2 pounds green rhubarb (about 10 cups chopped)
1 cup organic sugar
2 teaspoons grated zest and 1/3 cup juice from 1 or 2 grapefruits or 2 large Meyer lemons
Pinch of salt

Trim the ragged ends of the rhubarb. If large stalks look tough or fibrous, peel them. Chop them into 1-inch chunks, then put them in a 3-quart saucepan with the sugar, zest, juice, and salt. Cook over medium heat until the rhubarb has broken down into a rough puree, after about 20 minutes. Don't use the food processor—the look of the textured threads of rhubarb is appealing. Chill well.

Red Rhubarb Puree with Maple, Cinnamon, and Orange

Make this puree with red rhubarb the same way as the Green Rhubarb Puree with Grapefruit, using for flavorings 1 cup maple sugar or organic brown sugar, 2 teaspoons grated orange zest plus 1/3 cup fresh orange juice, 1 teaspoon ground cinnamon, 1/8 teaspoon ground cloves, and a pinch of salt. Serve chilled.

Baked Rhubarb with Vanilla, Orange, and Clove SERVES 4 TO 6

THIS SIMPLE WAY to cook rhubarb is the only one I know of that yields perfect, evenly cooked fruit. It will keep for a week in the refrigerator, to be called into play when needed. Breakfast might be one time—think of cold rhubarb and yogurt spooned over a crêpe, toast, or a slice of Yeasted Sugar Cake (page 242)—but it also makes a fairly instant dessert, served chilled with a splash of Grand Marnier and spooned around a vanilla custard or Yogurt-Honey Ice Cream (page 216).

1½ pounds rhubarb (about 4 cups cut up)
¾ cup organic light brown or white sugar
Grated zest and juice of 1 orange
One 2-inch piece vanilla bean, sliced lengthwise
3 cloves

1. Preheat the oven to 375°F. Have ready a gratin dish large enough to hold the rhubarb in 1 or 2 layers. Rinse the rhubarb, trim the stalks, then cut them into pieces 1 to 1½ inches long. A diagonal cut looks nice here. Toss with the sugar, zest, and juice and transfer to the gratin dish. Bury the vanilla bean and cloves in the rhubarb.

2. Bake until the rhubarb is tender when pierced with a knife, about 30 minutes. Remove and let cool in its baking dish; then cover and refrigerate. Taste for sweetness and add more if needed—a little maple syrup or a few drops of stevia will correct rhubarb that's a tad too tart.

Elephant Heart Plums Baked in Wine with Orange, Sugar, and Clove, SERVES 4 TO 6

PLUMS IN WINE with the scent of orange and clove make a fine baked fruit dessert—and an easy one, too, if you don't mind having the oven on in August. I single out Elephant Hearts here because not only are they spectacular red-fleshed plums, but they are one of the freestone varieties, which makes it possible to halve them easily and remove the stones.

6 large plums, such as Elephant Heart
1 heaping teaspoon grated orange zest
1/4 cup organic sugar
A small pinch of ground cloves
1/2 cup red wine or a Muscat wine

1. Preheat the oven to 375°F. Slice the plums, following the seam from stem to stern, then twist the halves apart. Dislodge the stone and discard. Place the fruits cut side up in a gratin dish or skillet that will hold them snugly.

2. Mash the orange zest into the sugar and cloves so that the sugar picks up the oils from the zest. Sprinkle it over the tops of the plums. Although it seems like a lot of sugar, plums become quite tart when cooked.

3. Pour the wine into the dish and bake until the plums are shrunken and tender, about 30 minutes.

PLUMS BAKED IN WINE WITH ROSEMARY
If you're intrigued by the pairing of savory herbs with fruit and sugar, in place of clove, scatter a few pinches of finely minced rosemary leaves over the plums.

ROASTED PLUMS WITH MUSCAT SABAYON
Make a sabayon (see page 36), using Beaumes de Venise or another Muscat-based dessert wine. Serve the warm plums with a frothy mound of the sabayon.

plums

ONE MIGHT THINK that plums are a difficult fruit as they receive comparatively little attention in cookbooks. Plus you hardly ever hear people waxing on about plums the way they do about peaches. It's for the usual reasons. Most plums are picked when they have color but not maturity, so they're tart and crisp—and not very likable. Also, the big, shiny modern plums have muscled the really good old varieties out of the market and almost out of sight. Aficionados worry, and with good reason, that some of our most exquisite plums, like the Santa Rosa, Coe's Golden Drop, or Elephant Heart, will simply disappear one day. Fortunately, there are growers, like Anthony Boutard and Andy Mariani, who are working to make sure that doesn't happen. Mariani will even ship his fruit to you overnight so you can have the chance to taste a real plum, properly ripened. While I don't advocate air-shipping fruit, I think it might be good to have the experience of eating the real thing so that you can hold it in your mind forevermore.

My husband and I recently had such an experience when Anthony Boutard filled a bag with plums and prune plums picked from his Oregon orchard and tucked them into the backseat of our car. Among them were Green Gages and a stunning Purple Gage, little Mirabelles, yellow-fleshed Senecas, the famed Prune d'Agen plus the giant Brooks, and other varieties, a rich tapestry of deep blues and purples, golds, greens, stippled with dots and blushed with pinks and patches of reds. Each fruit had a distinct flavor and a pleasing balance of sweetness and acidity. At last, here were true plums that left the corners of our mouths turned upward in big smiles. (Plums from Ayers Creek Farm can be bought at the Hillsdale Farmers' Market near Portland, Oregon.)

When truly ripe, not only do the acids and the sugars in plums meld in luscious harmony, but the fruit is aromatic and the flesh is plump and just a little firm.

In cooking, soft fruits are difficult to handle—they spatter and disintegrate and are just about impossible to cut into beautiful slices for a tart. But there are a few moments when plums manage to be both ripe and somewhat firm, and then, when cooked, the tannins in their skins become more emphasized. Indeed, plums aren't the easiest of fruits, but they can be extraordinary ones.

Despite their quirks and the challenge of actually locating good plums, when you do find them, plums have many uses in the dessert kitchen. In Germany and Austria they are traditionally sliced over buttery yeasted batters to make kuchens. They make incomparable crisps and, when sliced and arranged with care, handsome tarts and upside-down cakes. Plums are excellent when roasted with spices and wine and are harmonious with almond. Both brandy and red wine enhance these fruits, and for aromatics, orange, cardamom, clove, ginger, orange, and brown sugar are reliably excellent.

There are far more plum varieties than those dispirited "red" and "black" plums filling the supermarket. In fact, plums can be blue, green, crimson, purple, and gold, and many plums do have red skin or black. Some are heart shaped, others long ovals. Still others are spherical. As with all fruit, goodness lies in the variety, the place, the skill with which they are grown, and when they are picked. And ripeness is always the key to balanced flavor, so shop with your senses especially alert when it comes to plums. Even farmers' market fruit is often picked too green.

Here are some varieties to look for.

ALDERMAN: A plum I've found at several midwestern markets, this is a red-skinned fruit with bright yellow, juicy flesh. A very nice eating plum.

SANTA ROSA: Luther Burbank's superb medium-size plum with crimson skin and yellow-gold flesh is very juicy and aromatic. There is another that ripens later and is larger, called a Late Santa Rosa, but it isn't as good.

DAMSON: These blue-skinned fruits with yellow-green flesh aren't so easy to find, but when found, they are often favored for jams and jellies. They tend to be freestones, too, which is always an advantage.

SATSUMA: A small, round, red-skinned, and intensely red-fleshed plum that sometimes has skin flecked with green and purple. It is semiclinging—not quite freestone, but almost. The Satsuma was also developed by Luther Burbank.

KELSEY: Green-skinned (with splashes of red) and green-fleshed, this plum is often large and heart shaped. A very pretty fruit that can be sweet and firm at the same time, the Kelsey is often nicely perfumed, too.

ELEPHANT HEART: Here's a most stunning plum with red flesh and purple-red skin. Large, heart shaped, with red juice and sweet flavor. Spectacular, plus it's a freestone, which makes it ideal for baking halves.

MARIPOSA: Juicy and sweet big plums with greenish red skin and mottled deep purple flesh.

BLACK FRIAR: A dramatic big black plum that can be bland unless picked ripe. You might find them sold as dried plums at California farmers' markets.

LARODA: A gorgeous round, dark purple fruit with pale red flesh.

MIRABELLE: Tiny, golden plums with yellow flesh—too small to cook with but wonderful for eating out of hand. An excess of Mirabelles can be cooked into a plum soup, jam, or syrup.

Sautéed Plums with Cardamom SERVES 4

THIS QUICK SAUTÉ renders plums that are just shy of ripeness more promising than when eaten raw. Fruit that's stellar to begin with will, of course, be that much better. The tart, tannic quality in the plums' skins becomes more pronounced when cooked, but the sweetness of an accompaniment should put everything into balance.

Serve these with coffee ice cream, Yogurt-Honey Ice Cream (page 216), or a spoonful of mascarpone.

4 to 6 large plums in season, such as Elephant Heart, Santa Rosa, Black Friar, or a mixture
2 tablespoons unsalted butter
1/4 cup organic sugar or 2 tablespoons agave nectar
1/2 teaspoon ground cardamom
2 tablespoons Grand Marnier or 1 teaspoon orange-flower water

1. Rinse the plums, then slice them into wedges about 3/4 inch thick at their widest part.

2. Heat a 10-inch skillet with the butter over medium-high heat. When it melts, add the plums, sugar, and cardamom. Raise the heat and cook, jerking the fruit in the pan about every 30 seconds so that the cut surfaces take on some color, eventually caramelizing.

3. After 5 minutes or so, the plums will give up their juices. Continue cooking over high heat until the juice just coats the fruit and the smell of caramel is apparent. Remove from the heat and add the Grand Marnier. Then remove to a serving bowl, scraping in all the liquid from the pan. Allow to cool for at least 5 minutes before serving.

Pears in Honey Caramel SERVES 4

THOUGH VERY EASY to make, this dessert does ask you to pay attention to what's happening in the pan, because it will never be the same twice. If your pears are on the dry side, your caramel will form more quickly than if you're using pears that exude a lot of juice. Ripe Bartletts will cook more quickly than Boscs, and making this for two will be different from making it for four. It's all about adjusting for the needs of the moment.

I like to serve it as part of a cheese course, with a fresh tangy goat cheese or Cowgirl Creamery's Pierce Point, an exceptionally rich yogurt drained for an hour first, or dry Jack cheese. All work beautifully—and very differently from one another.

2 large or 3 medium pears, such as Bosc, Anjou, Comice, or
    Packham
3 tablespoons unsalted butter
3 to 4 tablespoons mild honey
2 tablespoons pine nuts
Pinch of salt

1. Peel the pears neatly with a paring knife. Cut them lengthwise in half and remove the cores with a scoop or a pear corer, including the piece that runs up to the stem.

2. Select a skillet large enough to hold the pears snugly. Melt the butter over medium-high heat, allowing it to brown a little around the edges. Add the pears, cut sides down, and drizzle the honey over them and into the butter. Slide the pan back and forth to combine the butter and honey, then reduce the heat to medium-low. Cover the pan, and cook until the pears are tender, 12 to 15 minutes, or until a paring knife inserted meets just a little resistance. Take a look after 5 minutes or so. If you have a pretty dark caramel by then—high heat and a thin pan will do it—add a few tablespoons of water, give the pan a shake to mix it in, then cover again and continue cooking until the pears are done, adding water again if needed.

3. Remove the cooked pears to serving plates. Raise the heat under the pan to medium-high and add the pine nuts and salt. If the pears have given off a lot of juice or the added water hasn't cooked down, cook until you have a bubbly, brown caramel, anywhere from 1 to 5 minutes. Serve the pears with the sauce spooned over them.

NOTE

You can cook the pears until they're done, say just before you sit down to dinner, then turn off the heat. Just before serving, turn the heat back to high and heat the pears through. Remove them to individual serving plates and continue with the recipe in step 3.

Roasted Mission Figs with Honey SERVES 4 TO 6

THIS IS AN easy way to enjoy figs that aren't dead ripe. I particularly like Mission figs here because of their dark purple flesh and skins, which roasting burnishes to a fine color. I serve these warm with just a dollop of crème fraîche slipped in between the two halves. This is easy to make for any number of people, from one to many.

12 to 16 plump figs
2 tablespoons unsalted butter
Tiny pinch of salt
2 tablespoons honey, such as lavender honey
Pinch of ground cinnamon

1. Preheat the oven to 425°F. Rinse the figs and pat them dry, then cut off the stems and, without cutting through the base, halve them from top to bottom. Set the figs upright in a dish just big enough to hold them snugly.

2. Melt the butter in a small skillet with the salt, honey, and cinnamon, then spoon it over the figs.

3. Bake until the sauce is bubbling and the fruit is heated through, about 15 minutes. Serve warm.

Nearly Candied Quince MAKES 2½ CUPS

FOR YEARS I'VE cooked quince on the stove, but lately I've come to appreciate roasting them until they're nearly candied. For one, the hot oven also heats my small kitchen when the weather is chilly, but more important, it takes less time for the fruit to become tender and turn that desirable shade of pink.

Because these candied segments keep so well in the refrigerator, you can use them over a period of weeks—even months. I often serve them with yogurt and a thread of the syrup as a very straightforward dessert. You can add the pieces to dishes that feature apples and pears in tarts, pies, crisps, and so forth. They make a pretty and harmonious addition to a compote of dried fruits, and are excellent paired with an aged Cheddar or manchego cheese.

3 cups water or 2 cups Riesling plus 1 cup water
1½ cups organic sugar
Zest of 1 tangerine or 3 wide strips orange zest
1 cinnamon stick
½ teaspoon cardamom seeds
3 cloves
6 large quince (about 4 cups peeled and sliced)
¼ cup late-harvest Riesling, Muscat, or other dessert wine

1. Combine the water, sugar, zest, cinnamon, and spices in a saucepan and bring to a boil. Stir to dissolve the sugar, then simmer over low heat while you slice the quince. Preheat the oven to 375°F.

2. Peel the quince, cut them into wedges about ¾ inch wide at the center, and remove the cores. Put them in a shallow dish, like a gratin dish. Pour two-thirds of the syrup over the fruit, including the spices. Bake, uncovered, for about 2 hours, turning the fruit every 30 minutes for the first 1½ hours and then more frequently during the last 30 minutes, as the syrup will be well reduced by then. You want it to caramelize and thicken but not burn. When done, the quince should be nearly translucent and slightly rosy.

3. Remove from the oven and immediately add the wine. At this point you can use the sticky, candied pieces as a sweetmeat or with a slice of cheese. To store them, add the remainder of the syrup and keep in the refrigerator.

Quince Braised in Honey and Wine SERVES 4 TO 6

IN THIS RUSTIC little dessert the skins stay on the quince (they disappear into softness), and you also leave the core of seeds intact and eat around it with a knife and fork. (The seed sections are handsome.) But if you wish to remove the cores, use a small biscuit or cookie cutter. Allow three ½-inch rounds per person, which is one large quince. Be sure to use any pieces that aren't quite presentable to add to tarts, compotes, ice cream, or other desserts. Serve with crème fraîche, Yogurt-Honey Ice Cream (page 216), or something else that's cold and creamy.

4 to 6 ripe, fragrant quince (about 2 pounds)
2 cinnamon sticks
½ cup honey
½ cup dessert wine, such as Quady Essensia Orange Muscat or Navarro late-harvest Riesling
2 tablespoons unsalted butter

1. Preheat the oven to 400°F. Select a wide, shallow baking dish that will comfortably hold the quince in a single layer with some doubling up if need be.

2. Rub the fuzz off each quince, rinse, then slice crosswise into rounds about ½ inch thick or even a little thicker, leaving the skins on.

3. Arrange the rounds of fruit in the baking dish. Tuck in the cinnamon sticks, drizzle over the honey, pour in the wine, then dot with the butter. Cover the dish with foil. Bake for 25 minutes, then remove the foil and bake for 20 minutes more. Turn the slices over and slosh the juices around, then return the dish to the oven and bake until burnished and tender when pierced with a paring knife, another 15 to 30 minutes. In the end the juices will have cooked down to a dark syrup.

4. Serve warm or at room temperature, alone or with something creamy; spoon the syrup over the fruit.

CHAPTER 5

· Classics You Can Count On ·

A crisp, a crumble, a cobbler, and a bevy of upside-down cakes are the classics I turn to throughout the year, all desserts that involve pairing fruits and toppings. Crisps place a topping over fruit, as do cobblers, their biscuitlike topping especially suitable for fruits that yield a lot of juice, like peaches. Upside-down cakes have it both ways—a batter goes over fruit that's lodged in a syrupy caramel, and then inverted so that the fruit is on top. True, there's not as much fruit in proportion to topping as there is in a crisp or a cobbler, but there are few desserts more certain to please. Upside-down cakes can show up at a family dinner or a company meal with equal success, and they can easily be made up out of fruit at hand, as the different combinations here will show.

Any of these desserts would be a good place for a young cook making a first dessert to begin. Even the one-bowl buttermilk cake that tops the Nectarine and Plum Upside-Down Cake on page 106 is perfect for the beginning baker and experts as well.

Apple Crisp with Cinnamon Cream SERVES 4 TO 6

AN APPLE CRISP always pleases. For apples use firm, crunchy types, such as Braeburn, Rome Beauty, or Jonathan. Or try the more melting Golden Delicious mixed with Granny Smith to make a sweet-tart combination. Gravensteins are excellent, too. Use them when you find them.

Apple crisp is good served with cinnamon ice cream, if you can find or make some, or plain vanilla. And cold cream is always good poured over hot apples. Flavoring whipped cream with cinnamon gives you a topping that's right in between.

THE FRUIT
8 cups sliced apples (about 2^1/2 pounds)
2 tablespoons organic brown sugar or maple sugar
^{1}/2 teaspoon ground cinnamon

THE CRISP TOPPING
1 cup all-purpose white or whole wheat pastry flour
^{1}/2 teaspoon ground cinnamon
^{2}/3 cup organic light or dark brown sugar or muscovado sugar
^{1}/4 teaspoon salt
5 tablespoons unsalted butter, cut into chunks
2 tablespoons walnut oil
^{3}/4 cup walnuts or pecans, chopped

Softly whipped cream
^{1}/2 teaspoon ground cinnamon

1. Preheat the oven to 375°F. Butter a shallow 2-quart baking dish and position the rack in the center of the oven.

2. Quarter, core, and then peel the apples. Slice them a scant ½ inch thick at the center. Toss with the sugar and cinnamon.

3. To make the topping, combine the flour, cinnamon, sugar, and salt in a bowl. Add the butter and work it in with your fingers to make a fairly coarse meal. Add the oil, work briefly, and add the nuts.

4. Put the apples in the baking dish and cover them with the topping mixture. Bake until the apples are tender and the top is browned, about 40 minutes.

5. Flavor the whipped cream with the cinnamon, and serve with the crisp.

APPLE CRISP WITH WINE-SOAKED FRUITS

Adding dried fruits makes a handsome crisp for winter. Toss the apples with a cup or more of dried fruits that have been cooked or soaked in wine, such as Prunes Simmered in Red Wine with Honey and Spice (page 147) or Small Dried (Dark) Fruit in Port or Pedro Ximénez (page 267).

An ad in an Irish magazine shows about twenty different apples. Each one has a problem. One is too round, another too long, a third too flat, a fourth too lumpy, and so forth. The end product that's free from all such characteristics is . . . apple juice! But all these so-called problems are what we love about varieties. A "sheepnose" apple has a long, pointy flower end. The Wolf River is enormous, blockish, and lumpy. A Reinette doesn't look like anything special, but boy, is it good for dessert. Even an everyday Golden Delicious can have the prettiest blush. That pale juice is not nearly as interesting as the different forms this varied fruit takes.

But I have a confession. Even though I'm all for diversity in edible plants, including apples, I am easily lost when it comes to America's iconic fruit. I definitely know some rare beauties because my father used to grow them—apples like Ashmead's Kernel, Golden Russets, and Cox Orange Pippin. I've heard that Northern Spys make a great apple pie, and I wouldn't hesitate to use them, but I don't really know them. I do know that the tart Bramleys (called *cooking apples* in Ireland) are great in baked desserts, as are the Wolf Rivers. As a northern Californian, I have high regard for the early Gravenstein and Sierra Beauties, while as a New Mexican of twenty years I now have a fondness for early July apples, the Transparents. But as for all the varieties that can be found in heirloom orchards scattered here and there across the country, unless they're right in front of me on a repeated basis, I've found it hard to build a taste memory of those varieties I don't see often enough to get to know.

Occasionally you meet a stunner. While driving through Vermont in early fall with a friend, we made a detour to an apple farm stand. (There were also baskets of highly aromatic strawberries, proving once again that these so-called early fruits can also run late in the season.) We bought two of each of many heirloom varieties, labeled the bags, and sat down to taste them. There was an unusual problem, though. The first apple we tasted, which none of us had ever heard of, a Holstein, was a spectacular apple with hard, crisp flesh, with such copious juice that it flowed freely every time the knife pierced its flesh. The initial flavor was tart and lively, but then it opened up and became round and sweet, leaving a lingering honeyed taste. It was so spectacular that everything else paled beside it—the Reine des Reinettes, a Macoun, the Cox Orange Pippin. All of these are fine apples, and they all tasted bland. But I'll never forget that Holstein, an apple I may never see again.

I've since come to realize that while that Holstein was truly a fine apple, we were probably lucky to find it when it happened to be at its very best, a rare little window of time. It was a little early for the Cox Orange Pippin, which would turn into an equally spectacular fruit probably a month later. And who knows about the others? In addition to variety, soil, location, and all of that, there's that tiny moment when all the sugars and acids and everything else in a fruit are in perfect harmony, and in some apples that might not occur until months after they're picked. What a complex world! No wonder it's confusing unless you've critically narrowed your focus.

What you need to know is that there are cider apples, cooking apples, and dessert apples. Some apples are crisp; others are soft. Some people like only tart apples when baking; others like to mix varieties so that they get a blend of tart, sweet, crisp, and soft. One really good pie maker I know prefers her oldest, most wrinkled apples regardless of the variety, because they have an intense, almost winey flavor. Others wouldn't dream of using such apples.

But sometimes a guide, even a very abbreviated one, can be helpful. This rather condensed one includes apples that are found at many supermarkets, but also some harder-to-find heirlooms, the farm stand treasures. Among the latter you're sure to come across some of the homelier apples from the Irish ad, most notably small, russeted apples that don't scream "red" and "delicious." But they are among the most delicious dessert apples you'll taste. The Pitmaston Pineapple apple, which I've found on several occasions and now *know* to look for, is another one you might easily pass by. But what flavor, and what perfume! It's why names are so important—perhaps you'll stumble across one, too, and give it a try. These are apples you slice and savor at the end of a meal, for dessert. But do keep in mind that much goes into flavor, including timing and, for most of us, luck. A cold-storage apple won't be the same as one closer in time to the tree. A tree-picked apple one week won't taste the same the next week.

Despite the naming of specific varieties below, in my opinion mixing varieties always yields a more interesting dish. And if I'm dying to make a crisp but don't have any of those apples listed, I just use whatever I have, and it will probably be fine.

FOR PIES, TARTS, GALETTES, AND KUCHENS: Golden Delicious, Sierra Beauty, Jonagold, Wolf River, Pippin, Pink Pearl and Pink Lady, York, Rhode Island Greening, Northern Spy, Idared, Cox Orange Pippin, Braeburn, Fuji.

FOR CRISPS AND PANDOWDIES: Granny Smith, Northern Spy, Braeburn, Rome Beauty, McIntosh.

FOR APPLESAUCE: Mixed varieties, including Gravenstein, McIntosh, Pippin, Mutsu, Fuji, Cortland, Jonathan, Bramley, Rome Beauty. Include some with red skins for their color.

FOR SAUTÉING OR CARAMELIZING: Sierra Beauty, Granny Smith, Cox Orange Pippin, Golden Delicious.

FOR BAKED APPLES: Rome Beauty, Golden Delicious.

FOR EATING OUT OF HAND: Cox Orange Pippin, Reinette, Ashmead's Kernel, Calville Blanc, Ginger Gold, Russets of various kinds, Pitmaston Pineapple, York, Liberty, Holstein.

A Hybrid **Apricot-Raspberry Crisp** SERVES 6

THIS IS A tart with a crisp topping that satisfies like pie. It's versatile beyond belief, as these variations suggest:

• Use blackberries, mulberries, or huckleberries with the apricots.

• Make the tart with sweet cherries (and a few pie cherries for flavor).

• Fill the tart with sliced plums tossed with the flour, twice the sugar, and a dash of something orange.

• Use pears, peeled, sliced, and tossed with nutmeg and organic brown sugar, or mixed with mulberries, fresh currants, or poached quince.

THE TART DOUGH AND TOPPING

$1/2$ cup almonds, with or without skins

$1/3$ cup organic white or brown sugar

$1/4$ teaspoon salt

$1 1/3$ cups all-purpose flour or 1 cup all-purpose and $1/3$ cup whole wheat pastry flour

8 tablespoons (1 stick) cold unsalted butter, cut into 10 chunks

1 teaspoon vanilla extract

$1/2$ teaspoon almond extract

1 egg yolk

THE FRUIT

4 cups ripe apricots, any overripe ones halved, the rest quartered

1 cup raspberries

2 tablespoons all-purpose flour

$1/4$ cup organic white or brown sugar

1. Preheat the oven to 375°F. To make the tart dough and topping, pulse the almonds and sugar in a food processor with half of the salt until fine. Set aside ½ cup and return the work bowl to the food processor. Add the flour and the remaining salt and combine. Add the butter and pulse until broken up into coarse crumbs.

2. Mix 1 tablespoon water, the vanilla and almond extracts, and the egg yolk with a fork in a measuring cup. With the machine running, add the liquid and pulse until the dough looks moist and has started to come together.

3. Remove ½ cup of the dough, add it to the reserved almond-sugar mixture, and set aside. Press the remaining dough into a 9-inch tart pan, using your fingers to build up the sides and your palm to flatten the base. If your butter was cold, the dough should be easy to handle. If not, refrigerate it for 15 minutes first.

4. Toss the apricots with the berries, flour, and sugar, then turn the fruit into the tart shell.

5. Rub the reserved almond-tart dough mixture between your fingers to make coarse crumbs, then cover the fruit with it. Set the tart on a sheet pan and bake in the center of the oven until the top is lightly colored and the fruit has released its juices, about 45 minutes. Remove and cool before serving.

Berry and Peach Cobbler with Corn Flour Cobbles

SERVES 8 TO 10

I DIDN'T UNDERSTAND why people got swoony about the combination of peaches and blueberries until I spent a few summers in the Northeast. When those local blueberries came in, along with peaches, they were indeed something to get excited about. Here in New Mexico we might be more inclined (or, rather, able) to use raspberries for our local berry. Elsewhere, the blackberry or huckleberry might be your best choice. Either way, the yellow corn flour dumplings end up surrounded with scarlet or purple juice.

I like to drop the topping by spoonfuls to get a cobbled look. If you prefer to roll out the topping and cut it into diamonds, circles, hearts, or other shapes, add another 1/3 cup flour or corn flour to make a dough that's rollable and easy to handle. I prefer it to polenta, which I feel is too coarse and hard here.

THE FRUIT

6 to 8 peaches or nectarines (about 6 cups sliced)
2 cups blueberries, huckleberries, blackberries, or others
3 tablespoons maple sugar or organic brown sugar
3 tablespoons cornstarch or 5 to 6 tablespoons all-purpose flour
1/4 teaspoon ground cinnamon

THE TOPPING

1 cup all-purpose flour or whole wheat pastry flour
2/3 cup corn flour
2 teaspoons baking powder
1/4 cup maple sugar or organic white or light brown sugar
1/4 teaspoon salt
5 tablespoons cold unsalted butter, diced into small pieces
2 large eggs
1/2 teaspoon vanilla extract
3/4 cup buttermilk or milk and yogurt combined

1. Preheat the oven to 400°F. Lightly butter a 2½-quart baking dish. If using peaches, dip them into boiling water for 5 to 10 seconds, then pull off the skins. Pit and slice the fruit, put it in a bowl with the berries, and toss with the sugar, cornstarch, and cinnamon. Let stand while the oven heats and you make the biscuit topping. *(continued)*

2. Mix the flour, corn flour, baking powder, sugar, and salt in a bowl, then cut in the butter using 2 knives or your fingers.

3. Beat the eggs with the vanilla and buttermilk. Using a fork or your fingertips, lightly stir these wet ingredients into the flour mixture until it is mixed evenly. It will be rather wet.

4. Transfer the fruit to the baking dish. Then drop the cobbler batter by small spoonfuls over the top, covering the entire surface. Bake in the center of the oven until the topping is golden brown and the juices are bubbling around the edge, about 25 minutes. Let cool and settle for at least 20 minutes before serving.

Right-Side-Up Cake

MAKES 1 LOAF CAKE OR A SINGLE-LAYER 8-INCH CAKE, SERVING 8

UNLIKE AN UPSIDE-DOWN cake, this cake and fruit combo lacks the extra sugar and butter that's so good (but oh-so-caloric), making a somewhat more subtle and lighter dessert. Use the batter for Almond–Corn Flour Cake for this cake; it's sturdy enough to support a layer of fresh fruits, be they berries, pitted cherries, huckleberries, slice peaches, quartered apricots, or cut-up (and even caramelized) pineapple.

The batter is made entirely in a food processor, which is why you start with butter at room temperature rather than cold.

1^1/2 cups fruit
2 tablespoons organic sugar
Confectioners' sugar for dusting
Almond–Corn Flour Cake batter (page 239)

1. Preheat the oven to 375°F. Butter and flour a 5 x 8-inch springform pan. Line the bottom of the loaf pan with parchment paper to come up the sides and lightly butter that as well.

2. Toss the fruit with the sugar and set it aside.

3. Follow the instructions for Almond–Corn Flour Cake batter on page 239.

4. Pour the batter into the prepared pan and smooth it out. Pile the fruit over the top. Bake in the center of the oven until lightly browned and springy when pressed with a fingertip, about 1 hour or slightly longer. Let stand for 10 minutes; then remove from the pan. Dust with confectioners' sugar. Let cool to room temperature before slicing.

A Yeasted Pear Upside-Down Cake

MAKES ONE 10-INCH CAKE, SERVING 8 TO 10

Ken Haedrich's no-nonsense country recipes appeal to me a lot. It was his idea to put a yeasted sugar cake over fruit, and what a good idea it is. This makes a light, fragrant upside-down cake that isn't gooey and isn't even very sweet for that matter. It's rather restrained as confections go, with a tender crumb and yeasty fragrance. The rising time is short, so this is not the equivalent of baking bread.

Definitely serve this cake warm with softly whipped cream if you've flavored the cake with cardamom, or with a cold sabayon (see page 36) made with Marsala or Beaumes de Venise, if not. This cake is a good brunch offering as well as a dessert, and leftovers are excellent toasted for breakfast the next day.

THE FRUIT

4 ripe but firm pears (1^1/2 to 2 pounds)
3 tablespoons unsalted butter
2 tablespoons sugar, organic light brown or white

THE CAKE

Yeasted Sugar Cake (page 242)
1 teaspoon ground cardamom (unless serving with a sabayon)
^{1}/2 cup all-purpose flour plus extra for kneading

1. Peel the pears, halve and core them, and slice them crosswise or lengthwise at least an inch across at the center.

2. Melt the butter in a 10-inch cast-iron skillet. Brush it around the sides of the pan, then add the pears and sugar. Cook over medium-high heat, sliding the pan back and forth every few minutes to turn the fruit and brown it on all sides. After about 4 minutes, turn off the heat. Arrange the pears so that they form a single layer in the pan.

3. Make the Yeasted Sugar Cake, adding the cardamom, if using, to the milk and egg mixture. Stir in an additional ^{1}/2 cup flour to make a soft dough that you can turn out onto a lightly floured counter. Knead it briefly until smooth, then press it into a circle the same size as the skillet. Lay it over the fruit and slide the skillet into a plastic bag to rise for 30 minutes. Then turn on the oven to heat to 350°F.

4. When the oven is hot, remove the bag and bake the cake until its smooth domed top is golden brown, about 30 minutes.

5. Place a cake plate over the top, grasp the sides with pot holders, and invert the whole thing. Slowly remove the pan. If any pears have stuck, lift them out with a fork and place them on the cake. Serve warm with whipped cream or sabayon.

Nectarine and Plum Upside-Down Cake

MAKES ONE 10-INCH CAKE, SERVING 8 TO 10

Alternating rings of nectarines and plums makes a beautiful surface that contrasts not only color but also tart and sweet flavors. Red-fleshed Elephant Hearts would be the plums to use, if at all possible, and I'd choose a yellow-fleshed nectarine, though you won't go wrong with a white one. Try to use freestone fruits if possible for their ease of handling. This batter contains a mixture of flours, including corn flour for its flavor, whole wheat pastry flour for its sturdiness, and cake flour for lightness.

THE FRUIT

4 tablespoons ($^1/2$ stick) unsalted butter

$^1/2$ cup plus 2 tablespoons organic light brown sugar

3 to 4 nectarines

3 Elephant Heart plums

THE CAKE

8 tablespoons (1 stick) cold unsalted butter

1 cup organic light brown sugar

Grated zest of 1 orange

1 teaspoon vanilla extract

$^1/4$ teaspoon almond extract

2 eggs, at room temperature

$^7/8$ cup cake flour or all-purpose flour

$^1/2$ cup corn flour

$^1/2$ cup whole wheat pastry flour

1 teaspoon baking powder

1 teaspoon baking soda

$^3/8$ teaspoon salt

$^1/2$ cup buttermilk

1. Preheat the oven to 375°F. Melt the butter in a 10-inch cast-iron skillet over low heat. Brush some of it around the sides, then sprinkle over the sugar. Cook for 3 minutes without stirring, then turn off the heat.

2. Slice and pit the fruits. Place the largest nectarine slices around the outer edge of the pan, curved side facing down and the pieces snuggled closely together or slightly

overlapping. Going in the opposite direction, make a ring of sliced plums. Then alternate plums and smaller pieces of nectarines in the center. Or simply alternate slices of plums and nectarines if they're the same size.

3. To make the cake, cream the butter with the sugar in a standing mixer until light and fluffy, 3 to 4 minutes. Add the zest, vanilla and almond extracts, and then the eggs, one at a time, beating until smooth. Combine the flours, baking powder, baking soda, and salt in a separate bowl. Add this dry mixture, in thirds, to the butter mixture, alternating with the buttermilk, with the mixer on low speed. Remove the bowl and use a wide rubber scraper to make sure all the flour is well mixed in.

4. Spread the batter evenly over the fruit with an offset spatula and set the pan in the center of the oven. Bake until golden, firm, and beginning to pull away from the sides of the pan, 35 to 40 minutes. Remove from the oven. Carefully run a knife around the edge of the pan to loosen the cake, then set a serving plate over the pan, grasp the two together, and invert. Lift off the pan. If any of the fruits have stuck to the pan, peel them off and place them on the cake. Serve warm or at room temperature.

peaches

THE MOST EMBLEMATIC SUMMER FRUIT if you don't count the tomato, a good ripe peach needs nothing, although sliced peaches covered with cream and a sprinkling of maple sugar are pretty special.

When it comes to baked desserts, these summer stars yield so much juice that tarts, which want a crisp crust, do not fare well unless coated with a layer of frangipane or crushed amaretti or biscotti. In general, if you're going to cook peaches for dessert, cobblers are the way to go, for they make use of all the juice the fruits give up without damaging the pastry. But you can skip the baking altogether, for peaches in wine are divine and so are peaches layered in a tall glass with a foamy sabayon. And the combination of peaches with blueberries, raspberries, and huckleberries is always good, whether you slice peaches into a bowl of raspberry soup or spoon warm huckleberry compote over peach halves.

When you do get around to making desserts with peaches, you have to peel them. When peaches are ripe, the skins will sometimes come off easily with a tug. If not, drop them into boiling water for 5 to 10 seconds, as you would a tomato, then transfer them immediately to a bowl of cold water. The skins should just slip off in your hands. If you're peeling a number of peaches, it's a good idea to remove them from the hot water and plunge them immediately into a bowl of cold—even ice—water so they don't cook while waiting to be peeled.

Peaches are clings (that is, the flesh clings to the stone) or freestones (they don't cling but separate with ease). The latter are a must if you want to have a full half of peach for a tart or for stuffing. You simply slice the peach around its seam, or indentation, and twist the two halves in opposite directions. This won't work with clings—these you have to slice.

Peaches can be yellow fleshed or white, and there are some rarely seen red-fleshed peaches (Indian Blood and Strawberry). We had access to an Indian Blood peach when I was growing up, and I've never forgotten the startling appearance of that deep red flesh.

White peaches, like Babcock or Belle of Georgia, are unsurpassed in floral notes. As for those flat fruits (Saturn, Donut, and Saucer), I can't muster much enthusiasm for them. They look tortured and strange to me, even though they can be incredibly good.

When shopping for peaches, ignore the allure of the color red no matter how tempting. Bring each fruit to your nose and breathe in at the stem end. There should be fragrance there to tell you that it's going to be good, even if it's still somewhat firm, but just a few days from perfection. If farmers picked them superripe, they'd be bruised, but there are farmers who keep those fruits for themselves, flick away the soft areas with their thumbs, and feel they've got the best of the lot.

Incidentally, if you shop for peaches (and other soft fruits) at a farmers' market, consider bringing a sturdy container to carry them home in. Understandably farmers are reluctant to let you walk off with their baskets, but many fruits, I've learned the hard way, will bruise if simply dropped into a plastic bag. Ripe fruit needs great care in the handling.

CHAPTER 6

· Country Pies and Tarts ·

Making piecrusts was long my nemesis when it came to baking. Yeast doughs and even puff pastry seemed far more approachable than forming a fluted double-crust pie. But there's no better way to get the hang of something than to do it over and over, and that's how I overcame my dread of piecrusts—I simply devoted myself to some serious pie baking over the course of a summer. It's also how I learned to press a consistently pretty good tart shell—by making a dozen a day for a year or so—the advantage of working in a pastry kitchen. Home cooks aren't usually inclined to make so many pies and tarts in rapid succession, which is why I've chosen the least intimidating and most straightforward approaches I know.

I was thrilled with the notion of the galette when it entered the scene. I think of it as a country pie, one that asks you only to roll out a piece of dough, then fold it freely around a chosen fruit. This means that your pie can be oval, round, or any irregular shape that appeals to you. Trim the edges and make them neat and even or leave them rough and ragged. You can also slide a big round of dough into a pie plate, add the fruit, and then fold the overhang over the fruit, making, in effect, a rustic double-crust pie, one I call a "fold-over" pie. If you don't want to fuss with cutting circles, matching rounds, and crimping edges, this is the method for you!

But the real stars in this chapter are the fruits that fill your chosen pastry. Following the year's unfolding seasons will give you a long list of fruit-filled pies and tarts to make. When a fruit is rare, I surround it in a custard of crème fraîche or cream. I also line some tarts with frangipane, a paste based on almonds or hazelnuts that sets off so many fruits to such great advantage that it has to be included. But always, it's fruit that dominates the dessert.

Often the fruits that fill these pastries are interchanged easily. Stone fruits can always replace one another or be brought together in the same crust; pears and apples also trade places with ease, as do different kinds of berries, which means that almost every recipe here can be considered a template. Like looking through a kaleidoscope where even a slight change in the viewpoint generates an entirely new and often dazzling image, so it is with fruit.

Apricot Fold-Over Pie MAKES ONE DEEP 9-INCH PIE, SERVING 8

MAKE THIS PIE when you have enough ripe apricots to make a real pie with the fruit more than a single layer deep. Instead of fussing with that top crust, you're just going to flop the excess dough over the fruit and be done with it.

The lesser amount of sugar leaves just a tad of tartness and is fine for those who enjoy some bite in their fruit. But apricots, like plums, often become more tart when baked. While the larger amount of sugar is definitely sweet, my informal jury of tasters says it isn't too much.

Chilled Pastry for Pies or Galettes (page 30)
8 to 10 cups pitted and quartered apricots (about 2^{1}/2 pounds)
^{1}/3 to ^{2}/3 cup organic sugar, plus extra for the crust
3 tablespoons all-purpose flour
^{1}/2 teaspoon ground cinnamon
^{1}/2 teaspoon ground cardamom or freshly grated nutmeg
2 tablespoons unsalted butter, melted

1. Preheat the oven to 450°F. Have the dough made, chilled, and ready to roll.

2. Toss the apricots with the sugar, flour, and spices and let stand while you roll out the dough.

3. Roll the chilled dough into a large circle, roughly ^{1}/8 inch thick. Drape it into a deep 9-inch pie plate, allowing the edges, which will be considerable, to hang over. For a more even appearance, trim the edges with a knife or scissors. Add the fruit and fold the dough over the top. Brush the dough with the melted butter, pouring any excess into the fruit, then sprinkle with a tablespoon or so of sugar.

4. Set the filled pie plate on a cookie sheet to catch any juices. Bake in the center of the oven for 15 minutes. Lower the heat to 375°F and bake until the fruit is bubbling and the crust is nicely colored, 40 to 50 minutes. Cool before serving.

Plum and **Walnut Tart** SERVES 6 TO 8

ONE NIGHT I made this tart, drawing from a bowl of red, purple, and black-skinned plums. The different colors were so pretty and the tart was so delicious that four of us ate what was intended for eight. For plums, look to Elephant Hearts, Santa Rosas, and Larodas for red and gold fleshed varieties; Kelseys for green. Using a mixture has the benefit of its contrasting colors.

One 9-inch Tart Shell (page 32), partially baked
1 1/2 pounds medium to large plums, ripe but still firm
   (see headnote)
4 teaspoons light brown sugar or maple sugar
1/4 teaspoon ground cinnamon
1/4 teaspoon ground cardamom
1/8 teaspoon ground cloves
Grated zest of 1 orange or tangerine
2/3 cup walnuts, finely ground

1. Preheat the oven to 375°F. Have the crust partially baked. Slice the plums into wedges a scant 3/8 inch across at the widest part.

2. Put the sugar, spices, and orange zest in a small mortar and work the zest into the sugar to saturate it with orange oil. Toss with the ground walnuts. Scatter 2/3 of the mixture over the crust and arrange the fruit over it. If you've no time for or interest in perfecting your arrangement, heap the plums into the tart pan. Otherwise, arrange the fruit in overlapping layers. Scatter the remaining walnut crumbs over the top.

3. Set the tart on a sheet pan and bake until the plums have started to release their juices, about 35 minutes. Remove and cool until slightly warm. Serve with crème fraîche drizzled over the fruit, or 1/3 cup each whipping cream and crème fraîche whisked together, sweetened with a little honey and a drop of orange-flower water.

Fig and Raspberry Tart with Honeyed Crème Fraîche

THE VERMILION JUICE of the berries will bleed into the cream, making for a somewhat garish pink and purple tart, but the acidic bite of the berries cuts right into the honeyed sweetness of the figs, and that's what makes these late summer fruits a popular pair. (Of course, black raspberries wouldn't do this.) If you don't like the looks of the red, dust the tart with a flattering veil of confectioners' sugar!

For figs, use ripe Adriatic or black Mission for their intense flavor and jammy interiors. Ripe figs are nearly squashy soft, and they needn't be peeled.

One 9-inch Tart Shell (page 32), partially baked
20 ripe, soft figs of mixed sizes, Adriatic or Mission
1 cup raspberries, more or less
3/4 cup crème fraîche or a mixture of crème fraîche and cream
1 to 2 tablespoons orange-blossom or other light honey
2 teaspoons orange-flower water

1. Preheat the oven to 400°F. Have the partially baked tart shell ready. Quickly rinse the figs or wipe off any dust with a damp cloth, then cut off the stems and cut them lengthwise in half. Arrange the figs in the tart shell, cut sides up, then fill in any gaps with the raspberries.

2. Mix the crème fraîche with the honey and orange-flower water and pour it over the fruit. Bake until the cream is puffed, about 35 minutes. Serve warm or tepid.

VARIATIONS

If you wish to avoid the cream, brush the tart shell with strained or seedless raspberry jam. Then drizzle a tablespoon of honey over the fruit before baking it. If you're looking for spice, mix a tablespoon of maple or organic light brown sugar with a pinch of ground cloves and 2 pinches of ground anise seeds and sprinkle the mixture over the top before baking.

the concord grape

A SEEDED SLIP-SKIN GRAPE, the Concord was developed in the 1850s, after a great many attempts, by a Bostonian named Ephraim Wales Bull. It was named for the village of Concord, as it first appeared there after winning first prize at the Boston Horticultural Society in 1853. It's hard to imagine such interest in new fruit cultivars in the general public today, but there was a great deal of excitement about the development of this floral blue grape. It became popular not only for its big, rich flavor and copious juice (it is *the* grape of grape juice) but because it is such a hardy plant. Developed on native instead of European stock, it could withstand New England winters. Whether because of its hardiness or gustatory qualities, the Concord grape traveled far from its Massachusetts home. My father took cuttings to California when we moved there in 1953, exactly a hundred years after the grape made its debut. Every September he made Concord grape pies, the pie that encouraged me to make pie dough, because once I was on my own, I couldn't imagine not having a Concord grape pie each fall. I've never missed a year, and I always manage to freeze some filling for a Thanksgiving pie.

Concord grape pies are often sold at midwestern farmers' markets. I have tried them, but they're never as good, it seems, as those you can make yourself. Maybe they're just too sweet for my taste. You can make one for yourself and see. The grapes you'll find at the farmers' market are often the best for pies, as they tend to be less watery than those grown commercially. They may be smaller, but they have more flavor.

Concord Grape Fold-Over Pie

"IT SOUNDS AWFUL!" a friend said when I described it to her, but she changed her mind once she had a taste. Concord grape pie has all the dense, fruity qualities of blackberry pie, and it never fails to please. It is truly America's own—and perhaps my favorite—dessert.

Use either white or purple Concords, but resist blending the two—you only lose the best of each color and end up with something muddy. I speak from experience.

Serve this pie slightly warm, with vanilla ice cream or heavy cream to pour over it. It's also rather interesting with cheeses, even the same cheeses you'd serve with apple pies—Cheddars and aged Goudas.

$1/2$ recipe chilled Pastry for Pies or Galettes (page 30)
3 pounds purple or white Concord grapes, stemmed (about 6 cups)
$1/2$ to $3/4$ cup organic sugar, to taste, plus extra for the crust
3 tablespoons quick-cooking tapioca or all-purpose flour
Grated zest of 1 lemon
1 to 2 tablespoons fresh lemon juice, to taste
1 tablespoon unsalted butter, melted

1. Have the dough made, chilled, and ready to roll.

2. Give the grapes a rinse. Pinch or slip them out of their skins, putting the insides into a saucepan and the skins into a bowl. Put the pan over medium heat, add $1/2$ cup sugar, and cook until the grapes turn white, about 3 minutes. Pass them through a food mill placed over a bowl to rid them of their seeds, then add the skins to the pulp. Taste and, if the fruit seems tart, add the remaining $1/4$ cup sugar while the pulp is still hot. Stir in the tapioca and add the lemon zest and juice. Let the mixture stand. The filling can be made a day or two before using.

3. Preheat the oven to 450°F. Roll the dough into a single large circle, then drape it over a shallow 9-inch pie plate. When the oven is hot, add the filling, then fold the excess dough over the top, making, in effect, a double crust, though it may not reach all the way across. Brush with melted butter and sprinkle with sugar.

4. Set the pie on a baking sheet and bake for 15 minutes. Lower the heat to 375°F and bake until the crust is nicely browned, about 30 minutes. Transfer to a rack to cool. As the pie cools, the filling will set.

CONCORD GRAPE TARTLETTES
If you have only a few bunches of grapes, use them to make Concord Grape Tartlettes. A 4-inch tart takes just ¼ cup of filling. Prebake the number of tart shells you think you'll need, following the recipe for the Individual Rhubarb Tarts on page 124. Remove the baked shells from their pans, fill them with the grape filling, and bake at 375°F for 25 minutes, or until bubbly. Cool before serving and the filling will set.

No Worries Apple Galette SERVES 8 TO 10

WHAT YOU DON'T have to worry
about is crimping a crust or
having one particular kind of
apple on hand, for many will do.
A really fine pie baker I know
favors her oldest, most wrinkled
apples for pies. They look terrible,
but they have well-developed
flavor that makes great pies. I
happen to love Wolf River apples
in pies, but I also like mixing
sweet or tart with crisp and
soft apples. Choose among (and
mix) Golden Delicious, Sierra
Beauty, Jonagold, Pippin, Pink
Pearl and Pink Lady, York, Rhode
Island Greening, Northern Spy,
Idared, Braeburn, and Fuji.

Apple desserts are always good
with a fine piece of cheese—try
Fiscalini's farmstead bandage-
wrapped Cheddar from California
or Pedrozo's Black Butte Reserve.
Gouda, especially an aged one,
would be a good choice, too.

Chilled Pastry for Pies or Galettes (page 30)
2$\frac{1}{2}$ pounds apples, mixed varieties or your favorite
3 to 6 tablespoons organic sugar, or more if the apples are tart
$\frac{1}{2}$ teaspoon ground cinnamon or cardamom
1 tablespoon cream, beaten egg white, or melted butter

1. Preheat the oven to 450°F. Have the chilled dough ready
to roll and a sheet pan lined with parchment paper.

2. Quarter, peel, and core the apples and slice them about
$\frac{1}{3}$ inch thick at the widest part. If the apples are on the tart
and firm side, make the slices a little thinner. Put them in
a bowl and toss them with 2 tablespoons of the sugar if
sweet, 4 if tart, and the cinnamon.

3. Roll the dough into a circle about 16 inches across. Fold it
into quarters, then open it on the parchment-lined pan.

4. Heap the apples onto the dough, leaving a 3-inch border.
Fold the excess dough over the fruit, overlapping it as
you go, then brush the exposed edges with the cream and
sprinkle with the remaining sugar.

5. Bake at 450°F for 10 minutes, then lower the heat to
400°F and bake until the crust is well browned and the
apples are tender, another 40 to 50 minutes. Let cool for
20 minutes, then slide the tart onto a serving plate. Serve
warm with a wedge of room-temperature cheese or a scoop
of vanilla or cinnamon ice cream.

Berry Galette *SERVES 6*

How can anyone go wrong with berries? If I lived in a place like Oregon, I'd be cooking with them all the time. Where I tasted this luscious pastry, however, was not in Oregon but in Washington, D.C., where a stellar selection of berries was lined up at the Dupont Circle farmers' market one Saturday. Ann Yonkers, one of the market's founders, made this galette for a farmers' market feast that evening.

Should you live where mulberries grow you can use them to make a berry galette as well. Mulberries, which grow on trees rather than canes or shrubs, have a flavor that is difficult to describe. It isn't exactly like any other berry, or any other fruit for that matter, but it's dense and berrylike. Serve a mulberry galette with crème fraîche alongside.

1/2 recipe chilled Pastry for Pies or Galettes (page 30)
3 to 4 cups blackberries, blueberries, or a mixture of berries
1/3 cup maple sugar or organic brown sugar, to taste
1/2 teaspoon fresh lemon juice
2 teaspoons arrowroot or organic cornstarch
1/2 teaspoon vanilla extract
1 tablespoon cold unsalted butter, cut into small pieces
1 tablespoon cream or unsalted butter, melted
1 tablespoon organic sugar for coating the pastry

1. Preheat the oven to 425°F. Line a sheet pan with parchment paper. Have the dough made, chilled, and ready to roll.

2. Gently mix the berries with the maple sugar, lemon juice, arrowroot, and vanilla. Taste and, if the berries are tart, add a little more maple sugar.

3. On a lightly floured surface, roll out the dough and trim it to make a 10- to 11-inch circle. Transfer it to the parchment-lined pan. Spread the berries over the pastry, leaving a scant 2-inch border. Distribute the cold butter over the fruit; then fold the edges of the dough over it, letting it gently fall into pleats around the berries. Brush the surface with the cream and sprinkle the sugar over it.

4. Bake until the fruit is bubbling and the crust is golden, about 35 minutes. Serve warm with heavy cream, crème fraîche, or vanilla ice cream.

berries and the boutards

LATE JULY, blackberry season, was the perfect time to visit Anthony and Carol Boutard of Ayers Creek Farm in Oregon. Midcareer farmers but longtime plant people and growers in Portland's community gardens, Anthony grows some unusual edibles that they sell at the Hillsdale farmers' market, and Carol is in charge of transforming their many acres of organic bush berries into the purest jam imaginable.

As soon as we walked out to look at the berries, it started to drizzle, but that didn't dampen the thrill of standing in front of dense rows of trellised canes covered with leaves, blossoms, and fruit. Unlike wild roadside brambles, which often yield only a handful of berries and lots of scratches, these long rows practically offered their fruit. I wandered down one aisle and then another, moving aside falls of fruit and gazing at heavy clusters of black, purple, and red berries, some still in flower, others ripening, and still others ready to eat and soon on their way to my mouth. I kept looking back to make sure it was all right with Anthony and Carol that I was eating so many, but they didn't seem to mind. This was my candy store.

Between bites, I took notes as Anthony had much to say about the different kinds of berries he grows. Blackcap raspberries, for example, those little blue-black, seedy caplike fruits with a lovely haunting flavor, are used to make the "ink" that's stamped onto hunks of meat by USDA inspectors.

Anthony also expressed great enthusiasm for the Chester, the thornless blackberry we were sampling. He described it as having a distinctively "clean" flavor, free of winey notes. It was an altogether delicious blackberry, and I'm thrilled to find that a few of our farmers in New Mexico are now growing Chester. He noted that commercial growers shy away from it and that it's hard to grow well. "There's no doubt that the Chester is one fussy customer, but for us it has always returned the affection lavished upon it. It's a great fresh berry out of the hand and freezes well to boot."

While the Boutards are definitely looking for flavor in their fruit, as commercial growers they also look for berries that do not turn mushy or leaky or lose color on hot sunny days. Chester has all these qualities, plus it's hardy.

Next we met the Triple Crown, a blackberry with thorns and a strong tie to Arkansas. Released in 1996, it is a relatively new berry. "The flavor reminds us of summer apples," said Anthony as he popped one into his mouth. He also told us that the Arkansas berries are known for their erect but very thorny canes and are usually released with tribal names, such as Apache, Shawnee, Comanche, and Navaho. "But because this one is only semi-erect, it didn't get a tribal name," Anthony commented. "Only the name of an equestrian triumph."

Anthony explained that fruits that come out of the Oregon breeding program typically have some native dewberry (*Rubus ursinus*) in their lineage, which accounts for the trailing habit and particular flavors. "Logans, Blackcaps, and boysens all have dewberry in them," Anthony said, "and with it that winey note. But," he quickly added, "in manageable amounts."

After the blackberries, we visited the raspberries (red, gold, and black), and after that the blackberry-raspberry hybrids that strive to combine the best of both parents. These include such familiar berries as boysenberry, loganberry, marionberry, olallieberry, and also tayberries. I had never seen a tayberry before, but the next day, in Portland, they were on the menus of three restaurants we visited, all the chefs devotees of Ayers Creek Farm. Tayberries are large, dramatic purple fruits, almost conical and very sweet.

Rain is the enemy of soft open fruits, like berries, spoiling fruits that are ready to pick. And just as rain ruins berries, so does washing them. There's no reason to wash them, particularly if they are raised organically, as Anthony and Carol's are. Washing just waterlogs the fruits, attracting bacteria, which bring on spoilage. Blackberries are trellised so there's no dirt on them. If dust is a consideration, simply dip the berries into a bowl of water, remove them immediately, and set them on soft kitchen towels to wick away the moisture before stemming them. Be sure to use them right away. Don't store them.

Lindsey's Austere Berry Tart

MY PASTRY MENTOR at Chez Panisse, Lindsey Shere, is a firm believer in the precept that less is more. Her raspberry tart, consisting of nothing more than a single layer of berries warmed briefly in their tart shell to tease out their perfume, exemplifies her minimalist approach perfectly. You need only three things to make such a tart—good fruit, the patience to arrange it with care, and a well-made raspberry jam or jelly to anchor the berries to the shell. And, if at all possible, you need to eat it within an hour of its making.

If you have to buy berries in plastic containers, buy an extra package, as invariably some will be damaged. Those who have easy access to berries can go with the round tart. But if berries are scarce, a long narrow tart pan that requires a little less fruit is handy.

Serve with a little sweetened whipped cream flavored with Kirsch or vanilla.

Tart Dough (page 32)
2 to 3 cups berries (three 6-ounce packages)
3 tablespoons raspberry jam or red currant jelly
Confectioners' sugar

1. Line a 9-inch round tart pan or a rectangular pan measuring 4 x 13 inches with the dough. (If using the latter, you will have extra dough.) Chill while you preheat the oven to 375°F, then line with foil and pie weights and bake for 15 to 20 minutes. Remove the foil, then bake until golden, 12 to 15 minutes more.

2. Lay the berries on a towel. Heat the jam with a few teaspoons of water to thin it, then press through a sieve. Brush about half on the tart shell. Starting with the larger berries, arrange them around the edge of the shell, working toward the center with progressively smaller fruits. Wedge them close to one another, making a single layer. Return the tart to the oven for 5 minutes.

3. Reheat the remaining jam, then dab a little over each berry. Remove the tart from its pan, set on a serving plate, and dust the edges with confectioners' sugar.

Individual Rhubarb Tarts in a Corn Flour Crust

MAKES SIX 4-INCH TARTS

THIS IS A dessert for a special meal—individual anything is always special—but it can also be presented as a single large tart. The puree can be cooked well ahead of time and the shells baked early in the day of your dinner. Then all that's left is to fill the shells and garnish the tarts with a perky little Johnny-jump-up or a cluster of local or homegrown strawberries.

This golden dough has character and crunch. Make sure you use corn flour and not cornmeal. If you can't find corn flour, use semolina. Like the corn flour, it has crunch, but not too much.

1 cup all-purpose flour
1/2 cup corn flour
1/4 teaspoon salt
1 tablespoon organic sugar
8 tablespoons (1 stick) unsalted butter, cut into chunks
1 egg yolk
1/2 teaspoon vinegar
1 teaspoon vanilla extract
2 to 3 tablespoons ice water
About 1/4 cup Rhubarb Syrup from poaching rhubarb, if available (see page 73)
2 cups Red or Green Rhubarb Puree (page 79), 1/3 cup per tart
Johnny-jump-ups, violets, or little strawberries for garnish
Softly whipped cream

1. Put the flours, salt, and sugar in the work bowl of a food processor and pulse to mix. Add the butter and pulse to make a large, rough crumb with chunks of butter still visible. Mix the egg yolk, vinegar, and vanilla with 2 tablespoons of the ice water and dribble it into the dough while pulsing just a few times. Add more water if needed, using just enough for the dough to be moist enough to come together in your hands rather than in the machine. Turn out the dough, gather all the crumbs, and bring them together in your hands.

2. Divide the dough into 6 pieces. Press each piece into a 4-inch tart pan (the bottom needn't be removable), working

it evenly up the sides, as you would with a larger tart pan. (You may have an extra ounce or two of dough.) Leave the bottom a little on the thick side. Chill briefly to firm the dough while preheating the oven to 375°F.

3. Line each tart shell with foil or wax paper, then fill it with dried beans or pie weights. Put the weighted shells on a sheet pan and bake for 15 minutes. Take the shells from the oven and reduce the heat to 350°F. Remove the paper and the weights, return the shells to the oven, and bake until pale gold and well set, another 5 to 10 minutes. Once they've cooled, carefully turn each pan over in your hand to release the shell.

4. To assemble the tarts, stir enough of the rhubarb syrup, if you have some, into the puree with a fork, leaving it streaky but still thick. Divide the rhubarb among the tart shells and smooth it out with an offset spatula. Garnish with a flower and serve whipped cream on top or on the side.

VARIATIONS

Instead of serving cream separately, fold ½ cup whipped cream into the rhubarb to make a fool.

Spread a layer of cream and crème fraîche whipped together in equal amounts over each tart.

Use the grape pie filling on page 116 in these little tart shells.

Cherry Tart with **Crushed Amaretti** <small>MAKES ONE 9-INCH TART, SERVING 6</small>

BINGS AND LAMBERTS make a handsome, deep red tart, but a jumble of red and yellow cherries like the blushing Rainier is fetching, too. A few pie cherries added to the sweet varieties would lend their essential cherry flavor. There is no cream or custard to hold the fruit in place, just a coating of warm red currant jelly. If the cherries roll off when you slice a piece, just stick them back on. This simple pastry is good with almond ice cream or the Yogurt-Honey Ice Cream on page 216.

One 9-inch Tart Shell (page 32), partially baked, dough flavored with $1/4$ teaspoon almond extract
$2/3$ cup crushed amaretti (6 to 7 pairs) or ground biscotti
$1^{1}/4$ pounds cherries
3 tablespoons red currant jelly, heated and strained
1 tablespoon organic sugar

1. Have the partially baked tart shell ready. Preheat the oven to 400°F. Cover the shell with the amaretti.

2. Rinse the cherries quickly, turn them onto a towel to dry, then stem and pit them. Heat the jelly with a tablespoon of water, stir to dissolve it, then pour it over the fruit and toss together with the sugar. Turn the cherries into the shell and press them close together. They will shrink as they bake, so don't be afraid to overdo it.

3. Bake in the center of the oven until the fruit has softened and turned wrinkled and dark, about 35 minutes. Remove. Serve warm, with ice cream.

CHERRY-FRANGIPANE TART
Spread ½ recipe Almond Frangipane (page 37) over the tart shell in place of the amaretti, then add the cherries, tossed first in the jam. This is an excellent tart, but then all combinations of frangipane and stone fruits do make the best desserts.

cherries sweet and sour

Rainier Cherries $4.00/lb

BRIGHT RED (but also yellow to nearly black), heart-shaped (but also round and even oval), and very sweet (except when they're sour), cherries are the cheerful fruit that heralds summer. They are one of the most irresistible fruits to eat out of hand. It's the tangle of stems that makes cherries fun to pick up, pluck, and then pop into your mouth. Once there, a bite of flesh should reveal a full, round sweetness with just the right acidic tinge to make the sensation compelling enough that your hands will soon be groping for more. During cherry season, which spans a period of six to eight weeks in most locales, I do little more than give them a rinse, then put them out in a bowl. Without fail, in an uncommonly short time nothing remains but the discarded stems and pips.

Of course, cherries, like other fruits, aren't always compelling. Too often they're bland and watery—okay, but hardly sensational. This state has to do with such things as weather, rain at the wrong time, variety, or an overzealous person stemming and washing them. When water gets into the flesh, the good juices come out, leaving the cherries bland. Best to simply rinse them, with the stems on, and then call it quits.

The range of cherry cultivation is wide, yet commercial plantings tend to cluster in the northern part of the country. Still, cherries thrive as far south as Virginia and Southern California. Generally, what cherries prefer is cooler weather than other stone fruits, and they hate a rain once the fruit is nearly ripe. While the trees themselves may be hardy, exterior conditions such as wind, too warm a spring, or disturbances in pollination make the cherry a more temperamental fruit to grow than most.

Harvesting also presents its challenges, for cherries are picked by hand. They have to be, because the fruits are best picked close to ripe, which means they're too fragile for a machine. And since their stems help keep moisture and flavor in the fruit, they shouldn't be plucked off. Perhaps this is why many cherry orchards are U-pick operations, where customers can deal with the ladders and pails and the labor of harvest.

Developed in 1875 and named for a Chinese workman, the purple-red Bing is the most popular sweet cherry. Not only is it big, sweet, and juicy, but it ships well, too, which makes it a grower's dream. We don't see the Bings right away, though. The early Burlats, the red-yellow Rainiers, the Vans (a Bing-like cherry), and a few other varieties come in before the Bings make their entrance. Others then follow to bring the season to a close.

At my farmers' market I've counted fifteen varieties over the course of the season, and this isn't even a cherry-growing area. Reading through *The Cherries of New York,* a compilation commissioned by New York State in 1914, I've become acquainted, at least on the page, with literally hundreds of cherries, a few of which can still be found today. Some we're likely to see are the red- and yellow-blushed Royal Anns and the pretty Yellow Spanish cherries, one of the oldest varieties in the country. We also see Hedelfingens, a German sweet cherry that's oval rather than heart-shaped; Sams, a dense, black-fruited cherry; and Golds, a rather small, clear, golden fruit that closes the season. The Golds don't look as if they would have much flavor—for many they don't even look like cherries given their pale flesh and clear juice—but they do. You might stumble across a Lambert, another great dark juicy cherry that's a favorite in many places. One year I joined people lined up ten or more deep to buy their allotted pound or two of Lamberts at the Missoula farmers' market, and it was well worth the wait.

Tart or sour cherries (pie cherries), which seem to grow everywhere but are raised for the commercial market mostly in Michigan, are what give cherry pies that distinctive cherry flavor. Even a handful, mixed with other cherries, will do the trick. They're tiny and fragile and not enjoyable to eat out of hand, but when cooked in a dessert, their flavor blooms. Snap up pie cherries when you find them and add a portion to a pie or cobbler or use nothing but. Gently squeeze them to remove the stones and forgo the cherry pitter. The premier sour cherry in the United States is the Montmorency. Morello cherries, of which there are many kinds, are another known variety, a deeper red than the bright-skinned Montmorency.

One-Eyed, Two-Eyed Gooseberry Fold-Over Tart

MAKES ONE 9-INCH TART, SERVING 8

IOWAN NEIL HAMILTON, who was with me when I found gooseberries at the Decorah farmers' market, asked, "Do you make a one-eyed or a two-eyed pie?" He shut both eyes tightly and made a sour face. "That would be a two-eyed pie," he explained. Then he demonstrated the not-so-tart version, closing one eye only and looking only moderately pained. I tasted a berry. I had the makings of a two-eyed pie, but only enough for a tart.

Even with a lot of sugar an aggressive tartness will remain with gooseberries. You don't want it to go away completely. It's part of their charm and character. But cold cream brings balance to the whole.

$1/2$ recipe chilled Pastry for Pies or Galettes (page 30)
4 cups ripe gooseberries
$3/4$ cup organic sugar
$1/2$ cup organic light brown sugar
$1/4$ cup instant tapioca
$1^1/2$ tablespoons all-purpose flour
2 pinches of salt
1 tablespoon unsalted butter, melted

1. Preheat the oven to 400°F. Have the dough chilled.

2. Rinse, tip, and tail the sharp little pointy ends of the berries, and rinse your hands to get rid of the debris.

3. Heat 1 cup of the berries with the sugars, tapioca, flour, and salt. At first it will be an unpromising mess, but in a few minutes the berries will release their juices. Simmer for at least 2 minutes to soften the tapioca, then mix with the remaining berries.

4. Roll the dough into a large thin circle. Drape it loosely over a 9-inch tart pan on a baking sheet. Add the fruit, fold the excess dough over it, brush the dough with a tablespoon of melted butter, and bake for 20 minutes. Reduce the heat to 350°F and continue baking until the crust is browned, about 30 minutes. If the juice has overflowed, carefully remove the outer rim of the tart pan and transfer the tart to a serving plate; otherwise, let the tart cool in the pan. Serve with cold cream.

currants and gooseberries

TRANSLUCENT, SMOOTH-SKINNED BERRIES of different hues, currants and gooseberries, both members of the *ribes* set, have nearly escaped me. They far prefer the steamy mid-Atlantic coast, muggy Iowa, or damp Oregon and cool Maine to the arid Southwest. Although I have carried home baskets of both fruits from all those places, my experience with these beautiful fruits remains scant.

Spare but cheerful, currants are arrayed in sprays on delicate branches, which is how they are usually sold. The shiny red ones are best known, but there are white and black currants, and even elegant pale pink ones that remind me of caviar, each translucent berry filled with black seeds. Currants glow as if lit from within and being so pretty, it's not surprising that they end up garnishing other desserts. They are still comparatively rare and expensive to use in summer puddings, but maybe someday we'll have them in such quantities that we'll actually start cooking with them. If you see some that have made a long journey in plastic clamshells, look very carefully before buying. Being delicate fruits, they can become bruised and then moldy.

Gooseberries are also something of a rarity, even though there are quite a few American and European cultivars, the latter being larger and sweeter, I hear. Like the pawpaw and the ground cherry, gooseberries were once far better known than they are today—they reliably show up in older community cookbooks, but now are rarely seen outside of farmers' markets. To most, they remain an unfamiliar fruit. Still, they have their fans, despite their almost mineral, harsh, rough taste in the mouth. Like rhubarb, they aren't everyone's favorite fruit, but those who love them love them.

Marianne's Peach and Frangipane Galette SERVES 6

IT WAS THIS dessert, enjoyed at chef Marianne Brenner's and Glen Hoffman's almond orchard near Chico, California, that reminded me what an extraordinary match stone fruits and frangipane make. Nectarines and all stone fruits, for that matter, can be used in place of peaches, and most other fruits can—and should be—paired with frangipane.

You might cover the frangipane with 1½ pounds well-sugared apricots, 3 cups pitted cherries, or 2 pounds sliced plums tossed with sugar. Pineapple—half of a small one, sliced thinly in wedges—is also divine over frangipane. And so are pears glazed with warm apricot jam and dusted with almonds. One of my favorite versions uses a mixture of fruits to make a tutti-frutti tart. People always ask for those slices that hold their favorite fruits.

½ recipe chilled Pastry for Pies or Galettes (page 30)
3 to 4 peaches, ripe but still a little firm (about 1½ pounds)
½ recipe Almond Frangipane (page 37)
1 tablespoon unsalted butter, melted
1 tablespoon organic sugar

1. Preheat the oven to 400°F. Line a sheet pan with parchment paper. Have the dough made, chilled, and ready to roll. Dip the peaches into boiling water for 5 to 10 seconds, transfer them to a bowl of ice water, then pull off the skins. Slice them into quarters or eighths.

2. Roll the dough into an oval or a circle 11 or 12 inches across and about ⅛ inch thick. Transfer it to the parchment-lined sheet pan. Spread the frangipane over the dough to within 2½ inches of the edge. Lay the peaches over the frangipane, then flop the edges of the dough over the fruit, letting it overlap. Brush with melted butter and sprinkle the sugar over the pastry.

3. Bake for 20 minutes, then lower the temperature to 375°F and continue baking until the crust is golden brown and the fruit is bubbly, another 20 minutes or so.

Three-Layer Almond Tart with Fruit Preserves

HERE'S WHERE SOME of those delectable market preserves come into play. You will not go wrong with apricot, raspberry, fig, or blackberry.

One 9-inch Tart Shell (page 32), partially baked
1/2 cup blanched almonds
1/3 cup organic sugar
1/4 teaspoon salt
2 large eggs, at room temperature
1 teaspoon vanilla extract
1/4 teaspoon almond extract
8 tablespoons (1 stick) unsalted butter, softened
2 tablespoons all-purpose flour
1/2 teaspoon baking powder
1/4 cup high-quality jam
1/2 cup slivered almonds or pine nuts
Confectioners' sugar for dusting

1. Preheat the oven to 375°F. Have the tart shell ready.

2. Grind the almonds in a food processor with the sugar and salt until very fine. Add the eggs and flavorings, process for another few seconds, and add the butter, flour, and baking powder. Process long enough to make a smooth batter, about 10 seconds.

3. Place the partially baked tart shell on a baking sheet. Spread over the jam, using an offset spatula, then pour on the almond filling and spread it out evenly as well. Scatter the nuts over the surface. Bake in the center of the oven until the surface is firm and golden, about 30 minutes. Remove and let cool to room temperature. Dust lightly with confectioners' sugar and serve this with soft mounds of lightly sweetened, whipped cream.

Wild Blueberry Tart in a Brown Sugar Crust

MAKES ONE 9-INCH TART, SERVING 8

LIVING AS I DO, far from wild blueberry territory, I'm thrilled to have discovered frozen wild blueberries—tiny dark blue spheres, not very sweet, but with that wild flavor. Since there aren't quite enough in a package to make a tart, I mix them with fresh cultivated blueberries and end up with a pretty jumble of big and little berries.

THE TART SHELL

$7/8$ cup all-purpose flour

2 tablespoons whole wheat pastry flour

3 tablespoons maple sugar or organic brown sugar

$1/8$ teaspoon salt

8 tablespoons (1 stick) cold unsalted butter, cut into small chunks

1 tablespoon ice water

THE BERRIES

4 cups wild blueberries, or a mixture of wild and cultivated, or one 12-ounce package frozen wild blueberries plus 2 cups fresh

$1/3$ cup maple sugar or organic light brown sugar

4 teaspoons quick-cooking tapioca or arrowroot

$1/2$ teaspoon ground cinnamon

$1/8$ teaspoon freshly grated nutmeg

2 teaspoons fresh lemon juice

THE GLAZE

Reserved juice from frozen berries, if you used frozen

2 tablespoons organic sugar

2 teaspoons Kirsch

1. Preheat the oven to 375°F. If using frozen wild blueberries, remove them from the package and let them thaw in a strainer set over a bowl while you make and partially bake the tart shell according to the instructions on page 33. Meanwhile, toss the berries with the sugar, tapioca, and spices, add the lemon juice, and let stand for at least 15 minutes.

2. Fill the partially baked tart shell with the berries and bake in the center of the oven until the fruit has begun to release its juices, about 35 minutes. Remove and let the tart cool nearly to room temperature before cutting so that the filling has a chance to set.

3. To make the glaze, simmer the juice—there should be about 2/3 cup—with the sugar until it has reduced by half, or to about 1/3 cup. Add the Kirsch. Then brush or drizzle it over the tart. If you used all fresh berries, sprinkle the Kirsch over the finished tart.

Silky Tart Dough

MAKES ONE 9- TO 10-INCH ROUND OR SQUARE TART

ONE OF MY favorite pastries involves this silky tart dough that's more of a batter than a pie pastry. Tender and cakelike, it's put together in a mixer in a matter of minutes and it doesn't need rolling. In fact, it *can't* be rolled.

8 tablespoons (1 stick) unsalted butter, at room temperature
1/3 cup organic sugar
1/4 teaspoon salt
3 eggs, at room temperature
1/2 teaspoon vanilla extract
Grated zest of 1 orange or tangerine (optional)
1 cup all-purpose flour

1. Butter a 9-inch round or square tart pan. Beat the butter with the sugar and salt with an electric mixer until light and fluffy, about 2 minutes. Add the eggs, one at a time, beating well. Scrape down the sides of the bowl and beat again until smooth. Add the flavorings, then the flour, mixing just to combine. Using a wide rubber spatula, scrape up the batter from the bottom, incorporating any stray bits of flour.

2. Scrape the batter into the tart pan. Using an offset spatula, spread it out, pushing the edges up the sides to make a rough rim. It needn't be very high—just enough to hold the custard. If the batter is extremely soft, refrigerate for 10 minutes, then finish shaping the sides.

Huckleberry Cream Tart
MAKES ONE 9-INCH TART, SERVING 8

THIS TART IS especially handsome baked in a square or rectangular tart pan.

Silky Tart Dough (page 136)
2 cups fresh huckleberries or wild blueberries
1 tablespoon arrowroot or 1$\frac{1}{2}$ tablespoons all-purpose flour
3 tablespoons maple sugar, rapadura, or other unrefined sugar
$\frac{1}{8}$ teaspoon salt
1 teaspoon grated lemon or lime zest
$\frac{3}{4}$ cup crème fraîche or sour cream
1 small egg or 1 large egg yolk
$\frac{1}{2}$ teaspoon vanilla extract
2 pinches of freshly grated nutmeg
Confectioners' sugar

1. Preheat the oven to 350°F. Lightly butter a 9-inch round, square, or similar-size rectangular tart pan. Make the dough, line the tart pan with it, and set it on a sheet pan.

2. Pick any stems off the berries, then toss them with the arrowroot, sugar, salt, and lemon zest.

3. Beat the crème fraîche with the egg, vanilla, and nutmeg. Scatter the fruit over the batter, then pour the custard mixture over the fruit. Bake until the custard has set, about 30 minutes. Remove and let cool briefly so that you can serve it slightly warm, the edges dusted with confectioners' sugar.

Cream Tart with Black Raspberries

IN NEW MEXICO I use our local red raspberries and blackberries now that a few farmers are growing them. But use whatever local cane berries you can get your hands on, including boysenberries, black raspberries, marionberries, and the like—Blackcap raspberries can be bought frozen and used that way or defrosted first. There is little juice.

Silky Tart Dough (page 136)
3/4 cup crème fraîche
2 egg yolks
1/2 teaspoon vanilla extract
3 tablespoons maple sugar or organic sugar
1/8 teaspoon salt
1 to 2 cups Blackcap raspberries or other berries

1. Preheat the oven to 350°F. Make the dough and line the tart pan with it. Make sure the rim is fairly substantial, although it needn't be high.

2. Whisk the crème fraîche, egg yolks, vanilla, sugar, and salt together. Pour the mixture into the shell. Dot the berries over the top and bake until puffy and pale gold, about 35 minutes. Remove even if it's wobbly, as the custard will continue baking. Serve while still a little warm and fragrant.

CREAM TART WITH PEARS

A classic winter dessert that pleases in its simplicity. Peel and halve 3 or 4 Bartlett or other pears (or use sliced poached pears). Remove the cores with a pear corer, then slice the pears crosswise a scant 3/8 inch thick, keeping the slices intact but not joined. Lift an entire pear half on a knife, set it over the batter, the narrow stem end facing in, then remove the knife and lightly push the slices to fan them forward. Repeat with the other halves, filling the shell as best you can. Pour the cream and egg mixture over and around the pears and bake.

CHAPTER 7

· Dried Fruit, Nuts, and Preserves ·

It's good to have a variety of dried fruit on hand. Often they taste better than their fresh but long-traveled counterparts and they aren't as tightly tethered to the moment as fresh fruit. Dried fruit, as well as nuts and preserves of all kinds, are some of the cupboard foods you'll find at the farmers' market. Not that you can't find them elsewhere—you can, of course, and some quite good products at that. For example, dried Blenheim apricots show up in some supermarkets, as do cherries and the big Red Flame raisins that used to be a unique farmers' market find.

However, the farmers' market is where you'll still find more unusual dried fruit, like dried Arctic Rose nectarines and Black Friar plums. You'll find jams and fruit butters made by artisans who work to reduce the amount of sugar in their small batches so that the big flavors of their carefully sourced berries, figs, apricots, ornamental quince, and bergamot orange come to the fore.

One of my cupboard shelves is chock full of bottles and jars of glistening jams and jellies that faithfully carry me back to Hawaii, Oregon, Canada, Vermont, Iowa, or wherever I've paused to taste a local honey or preserve and then committed to carrying it home. While I do consider myself a local eater to a large degree, I don't count the foods I carry with me as violating the local concept, if I've made a connection to the place. In fact, they are what keeps that connection—that awareness of other climates, people, and cultures—alive. Once we've met them, we know exactly where these treasures come from and what has gone into making them.

As for nuts, I have tasted, bought, and learned about varieties of hazelnuts, come to know the beautiful little hickory nut, revisited the black walnuts of my childhood, and learned about different varieties of pecans (including some tiny wild ones from Mississippi) and walnuts as well as the difference between a dry-farmed almond from Southern California and a plump, sweet irrigated one.

Desserts based on dried fruit and nuts, which are dense foods, always seem just right for fall and winter when the weather is brisk and cold, the same months that fresh fruit in their season are mostly gone.

Compote of Dried Farmers' Market Fruit SERVES 6 TO 8

THIS IS A dessert to brighten a winter evening. Consider the deep plum reds punctuated with dark prunes and the more delicate tones of white peaches and nectarines—gorgeous. The farmers' market is where you'll find such unusual dried fruit. If there are leftovers, dice them into small pieces and add them to grain-based desserts, such as the semolina pudding on page 180 or a rice pudding.

How long it takes for your fruit to swell and soften has to do with how dry they are. The current season's dried fruit cook more quickly than fruit you've had sitting around for a year or more, but eventually they, too, will revive with a little additional liquid.

3/4 cup honey or 1 cup organic sugar
1/2 vanilla bean, halved lengthwise
2 cups dried fruit, such as pears, nectarines, peaches, and apricots

1. Combine 3 cups water with the honey in a saucepan. Bring to a boil and stir to dissolve. Scrape the seeds of the vanilla bean into the syrup, and add the pod.

2. Add the fruit, reduce the heat to low, and cook until soft, about 20 minutes, or longer if necessary. When the fruit is tender, remove it with a spoon to a bowl, leaving any pieces that need more cooking to simmer until done.

3. Once all the fruit is cooked, simmer the remaining juices until syrupy and covered with bubbles, after about 5 minutes, then pour them over the fruit.

AN IMPROVISED COMPOTE OF DRIED AND FRESH FRUITS
The juxtaposition of dried and fresh fruit makes the compote more interesting. Build on it by adding fruit that have been poached first, such as quince or pears, or fresh fruit, including peeled and sliced Fuyu persimmons or a few sections of blood oranges or Asian pears, or by strewing pomegranate seeds over all.

Poached Dried Apricots and Cherries with Cardamom

MAKES ABOUT 2 CUPS, SERVING 4 TO 6

APRICOTS AND CHERRIES are so good together fresh. Why not bring them together in a compote of dried fruit? Serve with Greek yogurt or Cream Cheese Mousse (page 222), plus Cardamom Cookies (page 35) on the side. This compote will keep, refrigerated, for several weeks.

$1/2$ teaspoon cardamom seeds
1 cup dried apricots, such as Blenheim
$1/3$ cup organic sugar
3 tablespoons honey
One 2-inch piece vanilla bean
$1/2$ cup dried sweet cherries
2 tablespoons orange Muscat wine or 1 tablespoon Kirsch

1. Toast the cardamom seeds in a dry skillet over medium heat until fragrant, about 2 minutes, then remove. If the apricots are sulphured, drop them into a pot of boiling water, boil for 2 minutes, then drain and rinse.

2. Bring $1^{1}/3$ cups water to a boil with the sugar, honey, cardamom seeds, and vanilla bean. Stir to dissolve the sugar. Add the apricots, reduce the heat to a gentle boil, and cook for 5 minutes. Turn off the heat, cover the pan, and let stand for 1 hour to finish plumping.

3. Remove the fruit to a serving bowl with a slotted spoon, leaving the syrup in the pan. Add the cherries to the syrup, bring it back to a boil, and cook until it has reduced to about 3/4 cup, after several minutes. The cherries should be soft and the syrup slightly thickened. Add the wine and pour the syrup, cherries and all, over the apricots. Cover and refrigerate until chilled and you're ready to serve.

Prune, Quince, and Dried Cherry Compote MAKES ABOUT 5 CUPS

Simmered in wine, sweetened with honey, and perfumed with big pieces of tangerine zest, this compote is lovely served chilled with a late-harvest Riesling or a sabayon made with that wine. Once cooked and refrigerated, the fruit keeps for many weeks. I often dip into reserves and incorporate the fruit into other desserts, such as winter tarts and galettes or an apple crisp (see page 94).

The number of quince you'll need can be a little hard to gauge, especially if they're backyard fruits with flaws that require considerable trimming. Four medium to large fruits should yield about 3 cups. But there's no need to worry about an exact amount. If lacking in quantity you can add more dried fruits in their place or sliced firm Bosc or Anjou pears.

4 quince
3 cups Riesling or other white wine or 2 cups wine plus
    1 cup water
1/2 cup orange blossom, wildflower, or other mild honey
Several large pieces tangerine zest
2 cloves
10 prunes (dried plums)
1/3 cup dried sweet or sour cherries

1. Quarter the quince, cut them into wedges about 1 inch wide at the center, then slice away the peels with a paring knife. Don't be concerned when they start to discolor.

2. Bring the wine to a simmer with the honey, tangerine zest, and cloves. Add the quince, lay a piece of parchment directly on top, cover the pan, and simmer for 30 minutes.

3. Add the prunes and cherries and cook, uncovered, until the dried fruit is plump and tender and the quince are cooked through, another 30 minutes.

4. Using a slotted spoon, remove the fruit to a compote dish. Unless it is already thick and syrupy, simmer the remaining liquid until about ½ cup remains. Pour it over the fruit, cover, and refrigerate.

prune plums

PRUNE PLUMS, as distinguished from eating plums (although they make good eating, too), have drier flesh and more sugar, which makes them better candidates for drying than juicier varieties. The prune industry now calls prunes *dried plums* to make them more marketable, a ploy that has worked. Other plums can be dried as well, though with different results. I always look for dried plums at farmers' markets, where they are likely to be red and gold rather than blue-black, which makes them especially attractive in compotes.

The Stanley—a long blue fruit with dry yellowish flesh that separates easily from the stone—is often found fresh in late summer and early fall at farmers' markets, as are a host of different Italian and French prune plum varieties. They make handsome upside-down cakes and tarts. The Prune d'Agen is regarded as the *ne plus ultra* of prunes (I've seen them only once outside of France), although you can buy them dried in fancy food stores. In the interest of buying locally, however, I stick to California dried plums.

Prunes Simmered in Red Wine with Honey and Spice MAKES ABOUT 2 CUPS

CERTAINLY THERE'S NOTHING new about poaching prunes in wine. But I include this dish because I find that wine-simmered prunes are something I turn to often during the winter. I love them in a cream tart, spooned around ricotta cheese, with crème fraîche, or alongside a cake, such as the Brown Sugar–Ginger Cream Cake on page 245. In short, wine-simmered prunes are inexpensive, easy to prepare, and easy to incorporate into another dessert.

I don't know what ghastly new machine has been introduced for pitting prunes these days, but some brands look awful, all squashed with a big hole running through them where the pit used to be. Such fruit is best snipped in half with a pair of scissors before cooking. Or use more attractive-looking prunes—even those with pits. They do exist.

8 ounces pitted prunes (dried plums)
2 cups red wine
1/3 cup honey
2 tablespoons organic sugar
1 cinnamon stick
Pinch of cardamom seeds
6 peppercorns
3 wide strips tangerine or orange zest

1. Put the prunes in a saucepan with the wine, 1 cup water, and the remaining ingredients. Bring to a boil, then lower the heat and simmer for 25 minutes, by which time the fruit should be soft. Remove it to a bowl using a slotted spoon.

2. Return the liquid to the stove and simmer until reduced to about ½ cup, after about 10 minutes or so. Pour it over the fruit through a strainer to remove the spices, then return the cinnamon stick to the fruit.

3. Serve chilled, with cream or crème fraîche, or use in other recipes, as suggested in the headnote.

Figs in **Pedro Ximénez** SERVES 6 TO 8

PEDRO XIMÉNEZ IS that syrupy dark sherry that smells of dried fruits, sun, and molasses-tinged caramel. I cannot taste it without thinking figs, raisins, prunes, almonds, and fall and winter in Spain. Alas, it is not always easy to find. However, Shiraz is another wine you can use here.

These figs are so intense you really can't eat more than a few, but they're great to have on hand to serve with a mound of ricotta cheese, crème fraîche, or coffee ice cream. They are also delicious served with a thin slice of the Almond–Corn Flour Cake on page 239, and will keep refrigerated for weeks.

1½ cups dried white Calimyrna or Mission figs, or a mixture
1½ cups Pedro Ximénez sherry or Shiraz
2 tablespoons honey
Crème fraîche

1. Snip the stems off the figs. Put them in a small saucepan with the sherry, honey, and water to cover. Bring to a boil, then lower the heat, cover the pan, and simmer until the figs are soft and succulent, about 45 minutes. (Even though they'll feel tender when you press one with a finger before that much time has passed, they do need to cook for the full amount of time.) Turn off the heat and remove the figs to a serving dish with a slotted spoon, leaving the liquid behind. Cut some or all of the figs in half to expose their seeds.

2. Bring the poaching liquid to a boil and cook until bubbles cover the surface and the texture is syrupy when you tilt the pan—about 5 minutes. Pour the syrup over the figs, cover the dish, and let stand until you're ready to serve them. Place a few figs in individual small bowls for each person and serve with a spoonful of crème fraîche around them. Enjoy at room temperature or chilled.

Walnut-Pecan Maple Tart MAKES ONE 9-INCH TART, SERVING 10 TO 12

A NUT TART or pie is still expected on the Thanksgiving table, and this is my version. While I have put hickory nuts in the mix on occasion, they go largely unnoticed, a shame for such a costly little nut. Better to save them for another use.

In place of the typical corn-syrup custard, I've turned to maple sugar and maple syrup mixed with crème fraîche instead of melted butter to temper the sweetness. There's no avoiding the richness of a nut tart, but a little goes far. Let it cool completely before serving; then cut it with a large, heavy chef's knife to get clean, even slices. For the nuts, I use broken pieces for half the amount, then halves for the remainder, which decorate the surface.

One 9-inch Tart Shell (page 32), partially baked
1 cup chopped or broken walnuts and pecans
1 cup walnut and pecan halves
3 eggs
$1/4$ cup crème fraîche
$1/2$ cup maple sugar or organic light brown sugar
$7/8$ cup maple syrup
2 teaspoons vanilla extract
Pinch of salt

1. Have the tart shell ready. Preheat the oven to 350°F. Put the nuts on a sheet pan, keeping the chopped nuts and perfect halves separate, and toast them for 5 minutes, just to bring out their flavors a little.

2. Whisk the eggs with the crème fraîche and maple sugar, then add the syrup, vanilla, and salt.

3. Scatter the chopped nuts in the baked tart shell, then carefully pour the custard over them. Add the nut halves, with the rounded sides of the nuts facing up.

4. Bake the tart until puffed and firm and lightly colored, about 35 minutes. Cool well before serving.

Jam and Almond Tart or Bar

SERVES 6 TO 8

A LONG NARROW tart pan is one piece of equipment I use only rarely, but this is the recipe for that pan! I love its long rectangular shape partly because it's a change from round, but also because you can easily slice it into alternating triangles or crosswise into bars, giving you a tart or a cookie—hence the ambivalent name. You can also make this very easily in a 9-inch tart pan or pie plate.

A portion of almond butter, the kind you grind yourself in the market, replaces some of the butter normally used, underscoring the almond flavor, just the thing for showcasing the summer's preserves.

8 tablespoons (1 stick) unsalted butter, softened
2 ounces ground almond butter
1/2 cup confectioners' sugar
1 tablespoon organic sugar
1/8 teaspoon salt
1/4 teaspoon almond extract
1 egg yolk
1 cup all-purpose flour
1/2 to 3/4 cup jam, such as fig, apricot, blackberry, or raspberry
1/3 cup sliced almonds or pine nuts

1. Preheat the oven to 325°F. Beat the butter and almond butter together until smooth. Stir in the sugars, salt, almond extract, and the egg yolk, then stir in the flour. Work the dough briefly with your hands. If it doesn't all come together, don't worry. The crumbs will be used.

2. Press the dough into the tart pan, working it up the sides. Try to get the base even. Spread the jam over the dough, then scatter any remaining crumbs over the top. Lightly press the almonds into the jam.

3. Bake in the center of the oven until golden, about 30 minutes. Set the warm tart on a jar, allowing the sides to drop off. Then, using a sharp knife, cut the tart into triangular pieces, wedges, or bars.

Fresh and Dried Cranberry, Orange, and Walnut Tart

MAKES ONE 9-INCH TART, SERVING 8 TO 10

TART TASTING, FRESH, and filled with spice, this winter tart has an almost candylike texture.

One 9-inch Tart Shell (page 32), partially baked, dough flavored with grated citrus zest
1 cup unsweetened dried cranberries
3 cups (one 12-ounce bag) fresh cranberries
$1/4$ orange with skin, thinly sliced, plus juice of the remainder of the orange
1 cup organic brown sugar or maple sugar or $1/2$ cup agave nectar
1 teaspoon ground cinnamon
$1/8$ teaspoon ground cloves
2 teaspoons all-purpose flour
1 cup finely chopped pecans or walnuts
1 tablespoon unsalted butter
1 tablespoon orange liqueur or orange-flower water
Softly whipped cream or crème fraîche

1. Preheat the oven to 375°F. Have the tart shell ready to fill and set on a cookie sheet.

2. Cover the dried cranberries with warm water and set aside while you gather your ingredients. Then drain and put them in a 3-quart saucepan with the fresh cranberries, orange slices, orange juice, and sugar. Cook over medium-high heat, stirring occasionally, until the cranberries have popped and released their juices, about 12 minutes.

3. Stir in the cinnamon, cloves, and flour and cook for 1 minute more. Add the nuts and remove from the heat. Taste for sweetness and add more sugar or agave nectar, if needed.

4. Add the filling to the tart shell. Dot the butter over the top, then cover lightly with parchment or foil. Bake in the center of the oven for 35 minutes. Remove the foil and spoon 1 tablespoon orange liqueur over the top. Serve at room temperature with whipped cream or crème fraîche.

three related nuts

IF YOU WERE TO EXTRACT two perfect halves each from a pecan, walnut, and hickory nut, you would see that they resemble each other the way relatives do—they are indeed similar, but also different. The walnut meat is large and plump and honey-colored; the pecan is longer, flatter, and reddish; the hickory nut is the smallest of all, and also lightly colored, each half beautifully flared. While all have wrinkled grooves running down their length, their shapes, shells, and sizes differ. All are members of the same botanical family.

The pecan is native to the southern part of the country. Long collected by natives from wild stands, the Spanish organized the trees into orchards and today there are all kinds of pecan cultivars. At a pecan orchard in Texas I saw short nuts, long ones, varieties the owners said were rare, and others they said were "the best." Inch-long wild Missouri pecans can sometimes be found in farmers' markets. All pecans are very tasty, especially when roasted lightly.

The black shaggy bark of the aptly named shagbark hickory gives it a dark and foreboding appearance, especially if you encounter it without its leaves, standing with sinister authority in a midwestern forest. The shagbark hickory is not rare—it's one of the most abundant of North American nut trees—but its tiny, buttery kernels are hard to come by. They're tough to crack and extract, and the effort involved in bringing them to an edible form is considerable. This is what makes them a rare find and rather expensive. Once found, though, you'll have the most exquisite morsels.

dates

DATES' HOME IN THE WORLD is limited to a narrow band of thirty-five degrees latitude. And not all lands within that band are hospitable to date palms. In fact, much of that area isn't land at all, but ocean. Some of the countries where dates thrive are Algeria, Morocco, Tunisia, Iraq, Iran, Libya, Jordan, parts of Spain, and a small area in the United States around Phoenix and in Palm Desert.

Date palms require two things: for their heads to be dry and their feet to be wet. Even mild humidity is a disaster for dates, but there's got to be plenty of water underneath the crust of desert soil if they're to survive. Like gigantic straws, date palms drink heavily from the ground, drawing and filtering the water up through their trunks, which, when fully mature, can soar skyward to a height of sixty or seventy feet.

While date gardens have a calm and stately appearance, dates require a lot of fussing, which is one of the reasons they're expensive. The trees have to be pruned, trimmed, and pollinated; date clusters have to be sheltered from blowing sand and then harvested. To save on labor, some growers wait until the last fruits have ripened before picking, by which time some will have become dried and hard, like grapes that have turned to raisins. It's easier for the pickers, since the dates are less sticky and the job gets done in one pass, but some gardens pick the dates as they ripen. Douglas Adair, the owner of Pato's Dream Date Farm, who makes many pickings, says about his Medjools, "We'll have dates so soft you can hardly handle them without mashing them." These dates, which really do melt in your mouth, end up in little cups and trays at farmers' markets in Southern California.

Mostly the dates we buy are cured and somber-hued, but when fresh they are bright yellow, pale gold, greenish, and even red before yielding their brightness to more dark and durable shades. In October one can sometimes find them on the stem, in their *rutab*—Arabic for "wet"—state. They're yellow when you buy them, but as they turn brown they become very moist and juicy. Eaten chilled, they are soft, messy, and stunningly good.

There are three basic types of dates: moist, semidry, and dry. A moist, soft date, like the Medjool, is a dessert date. The Deglet Noor and Zahidi are two examples of semidry dates. Although moist and sugary, they hold their shape and texture when baked. Use a mix of moist and semidry dates together in a date pudding or cake and you'll get melting pockets and discrete pieces of fruit. Semidry dates are excellent for eating out of hand or for stuffing with almond paste.

Dates you can put in your pocket for a hike without having to wrap them in anything are called *dry dates*. They're nourishing and chewy, but not a date you'd serve for dessert.

Minced Dried Fruit and Spice Tart

MAKES ONE 9-INCH TART, SERVING 10 TO 12

DRIED FRUITS WITH a hint of lemon and the taste of sherry make a dessert that's destined for the winter table. The minute you add the spices, you can't help thinking "mincemeat."

I love the look of the distinct pieces of dried fruits with their different colors and the exposed seeds of the figs. But there has to be a way for the pieces to adhere, or the tart will just fall apart when cut. Pureeing a portion of the fruit does the work of binding the filling perfectly. Because the filling is dense and not overly moist, you don't have to prebake the tart shell. Serve with the flavored sour cream spread over the top or on the side.

1 chilled 9-inch tart shell made from Tart Dough (page 32)
3 cups mixed dried fruits, including figs, prunes, Red Flame raisins, green or golden raisins, and currants
Grated zest of 1 large lemon
1 tablespoon fresh lemon juice
$1/3$ cup organic brown sugar or 3 tablespoons agave nectar
$1/2$ teaspoon ground cinnamon
$1/4$ teaspoon freshly grated nutmeg
$1/8$ teaspoon ground cloves
$1/8$ teaspoon salt
$1/2$ teaspoon orange-flower water
1 tablespoon unsalted butter
2 tablespoons arrowroot dissolved in $1/3$ cup sherry or whiskey
$3/4$ cup lightly toasted walnuts or pecans, finely chopped
1 cup sour cream or crème fraîche
1 tablespoon organic sugar or honey
$1/2$ teaspoon vanilla extract

1. Preheat the oven to 375°F. Have the tart shell made and chilled. Using a knife or scissors dipped in flour, snip the fruits into small pieces, about the size of corn kernels.

2. Cover the fruits with boiling water and let stand for 5 minutes or longer to soften. Set aside ½ cup of the liquid, then drain the fruit. Put a third of it into a blender or food processor and make a rough puree with the reserved liquid. Transfer the puree to a saucepan with the rest of the fruit. Add the lemon zest, juice, sugar, spices, salt, orange-flower

water, and butter. Cook over medium heat, stirring frequently, for 4 minutes. Then stir in the arrowroot mixture and cook until clear, another 30 seconds or so. The mixture should look moist and shiny. Stir in the nuts.

3. Add the filling to the tart shell and even it out. Bake until the crust is browned, about 35 minutes. Cool to room temperature before slicing.

4. Combine the sour cream, sugar, and vanilla. Either spread it over the cooled tart just before serving or serve each slice with a generous spoonful on the side.

Walnut or Pecan Torte with Blackberry Preserves

DEEP, FRUITY BLACKBERRY or black raspberry preserves make a good match with these nuts and the espresso-flavored whipped cream that goes on the side. Wrap any leftovers of this light, airy cake well so it doesn't dry out.

Potato starch is available through Bob's Red Mill.

1 cup walnuts or pecan meats
$^{3}/_{4}$ cup organic white or light brown sugar
4 eggs, at room temperature, separated
$^{1}/_{2}$ teaspoon salt
$^{1}/_{4}$ teaspoon cream of tartar
$1^{1}/_{2}$ teaspoons vanilla extract
1 cup sifted potato starch or cake flour
$^{1}/_{2}$ cup blackberry, Blackcap raspberry, or apricot jam
Confectioners' sugar for dusting
Softly whipped cream flavored with finely ground or cold brewed espresso

1. Preheat the oven to 350°F. Butter and flour a 9-inch springform pan or dust the buttered tin with fine bread crumbs.

2. For the finest texture, grind the walnuts by hand in a handheld nut grinder, which will give them a light, feathery texture. Lacking that, pulse them in a food processor with a tablespoon of the sugar. Walnut meats are very soft, so take care that you don't turn them into nut butter.

3. Whisk the egg whites in the bowl of an electric mixer with half the salt and the cream of tartar on medium speed until foamy. Raise the speed to medium-high, gradually

add 3 tablespoons of the sugar, and whisk until the whites are firm but moist, forming glossy peaks that aren't too stiff. Scrape them into a large bowl.

4. Without rinsing out the mixing bowl, add the yolks, the remaining sugar, the vanilla, and the remaining salt and beat on high speed until light yellow and thick, about 4 minutes. Reduce the speed to low and add the potato starch in 4 parts. Stop and scrape down the sides of the bowl and around the bottom, making sure everything is incorporated.

5. Scoop about a quarter of the egg whites into the yolk mixture and stir to loosen the texture. Then pour the lightened yolks over the remaining whites, fold a few times, and scatter the walnuts over the top. Fold quickly until everything is blended evenly. Pour the batter into the prepared pan and bake in the center of the oven until risen, golden brown, and a cake tester comes out clean, 25 to 30 minutes. Let the cake cool in the pan.

6. Release the form and separate the cake from the bottom of the pan. Slice it crosswise in half. Spread the bottom layer with jam, return the top layer, and place on a cake plate. Dust with confectioners' sugar and serve with the coffee flavored whipped cream.

Pistachio-Cardamom Torte

with Warm Cherry Compote MAKES ONE 9-INCH TORTE, SERVING 8 TO 10

ALTHOUGH A NUT torte might sound wintry, this is a cake to keep in mind for a June birthday, when the delectable little pie cherries are in season. Or, in winter, you could serve it with a sauce of dried cherries in wine. With or without the cherries, the cake is delicious served simply with lightly sweetened whipped cream.

1 cup unsalted hulled pistachio nuts
1 cup organic sugar
1 teaspoon freshly ground cardamom
3/4 cup sifted cake flour
6 eggs, at room temperature, 5 separated
1/4 teaspoon salt
1/2 teaspoon cream of tartar
Grated zest of 1 orange or tangerine
2 teaspoons orange-flower or rose water

TO FINISH
2 tablespoons unsalted hulled pistachio nuts
3 tablespoons red currant or rose petal jam
Fresh Cherry Compote (page 261) or Dried Cherries in Red Wine (page 266)
1 cup cream, softly whipped and lightly sweetened

1. Preheat the oven to 325°F. Butter and flour a 9-inch springform pan. Pulse the pistachios in a food processor with 1 tablespoon of the sugar, the cardamom, and the flour until the texture is fine, being careful not to make pistachio butter.

2. Whip the 5 egg whites in the bowl of an electric mixer with the salt and cream of tartar on medium speed until foamy. Raise the speed to medium-high and beat, slowly adding half of the remaining sugar, 1 tablespoon at a time, until thick and glossy. The whites should be firm but not stiff, drooping just slightly at the tips when you hold your

whisk sideways. Finally, stir in the orange zest and orange-flower water. Scrape the whites into a large bowl.

3. Without rinsing anything, put the 5 yolks, the whole egg, and the remaining sugar into the bowl and beat at high speed until pale and thick, and a ribbon holds its shape for a second, about 4 minutes. Scrape the yolks over the whites and fold them together with a large rubber spatula, using no more than 8 strokes. Don't try to get everything perfectly blended—you don't want to lose volume.

4. Scatter on about a fourth of the nut mixture and fold it in. Continue adding and folding in the nut mixture a fourth at a time, using only 4 or 5 strokes per addition. Be sure to cut through the middle to break up any clumps of flour.

5. Scrape the batter into the pan and bake in the center of the oven until golden and pulling away from the sides, about 35 minutes. Remove from the oven, loosen the sides, and let the cake cool in the pan.

6. Finely chop the 2 tablespoons of pistachios. Melt the jam in a small saucepan, brush it over the top of the cake, then scatter on the nuts. Serve the cake with a spoonful of the cherry compote or dried cherries in wine and a spoonful of softly whipped cream.

MEDJOOL DATES
with Citrus and Walnuts

∾

Dates are fresh and moist during the winter months, the same months that citrus fruits are at their best. Medjools are the largest, softest, and, to my mind, most delicious of all the many date varieties. Enjoy dates with easy-to-peel citrus fruits, the late Pixie tangerines, Clementines, or other tangerines. If using oranges, either score the skin first so that they're easy to peel or peel sections of the fruits and then arrange them on a plate with dates. Pomelo sections and semidry dates, like Deglet Noor, make a subtle, slightly less sweet pairing.

Walnuts, set out with a cracker or already cracked into large pieces, mediate between the sweetness of the dates and citrus. For that matter, you might also include some dark chocolate or chocolate bark, nut brittle, and other sweets. What a pleasing succession of tastes and textures can be found here—a bite of soft sweet date, followed by a crunchy nut, then a sweet, juicy section of citrus.

A Not-Quite-So-Sticky Pudding SERVES 8

Super-sticky desserts aren't my cup of tea, but I do like a date pudding, and if I did want a major sweet, this would be the one. Pouring hot liquid over a thick batter never looks as if it's going to work in puddings of this type, but magically, it does. You end up with a tender puddinglike cake surrounded by a dark molten sauce.

I use coffee in place of some of the usual water for the sauce. I like the flavor of coffee with dates, and its bitterness helps temper their sweetness. There's less sugar than is typically called for, but still plenty. Douse the finished cake with brandy, Marsala, or Kahlúa and serve warm with something cold and creamy—like coffee ice cream or chilled heavy cream.

8 ounces whole dates (about 1 1/2 cups)
1 cup all-purpose or whole wheat pastry flour
1/2 cup plus 2 tablespoons light muscovado or organic brown sugar
2 teaspoons baking powder
1/2 teaspoon salt
1 cup chopped walnuts
1/2 cup buttermilk or milk
2 tablespoons toasted walnut oil or unsalted butter, melted
1/2 cup strong brewed coffee
2 tablespoons unsalted butter
2/3 cup dark muscovado or dark brown sugar
2 tablespoons brandy, Marsala, or Kahlúa

1. Preheat the oven to 350°F. Have ready a 2-quart baking dish. If the dates are hard, steam them for a few minutes over simmering water to soften, then cool and pit them. Chop each date into about 6 pieces. You should have about 1 cup packed.

2. Combine the flour, light muscovado sugar, baking powder, and salt in a bowl and stir together. Add the dates, nuts, buttermilk, and oil and mix together to make a thick batter. You may find that your hands are the best tools for this. Pat the batter into the baking dish.

3. Bring the coffee, 1 cup water, the butter, and the dark muscovado sugar to a boil. Stir to dissolve the sugar and melt the butter. Pour the liquid over the batter, then bake for 30 minutes. A gooey sauce will puddle up around the edges. Pour the alcohol over the hot cake. Serve warm with cold heavy cream or ice cream.

Winter Squash Cake with Dates MAKES ONE 9-INCH CAKE, SERVING 10 TO 12

THIS LARGE, MOIST cake is studded with dates and sweetened with maple syrup. While it's easily transformed into a spice cake (see the variation), you might find, as I do, that the subtle flavors of the squash, maple, and date are more clearly perceived without the spice.

I like this cold-weather cake served with maple yogurt, Yogurt-Honey Ice Cream (page 216) plus a drizzle of Apple Cider Syrup (page 252), or warm maple syrup.

2 cups all-purpose flour or mixed whole wheat flour and all-purpose flour

2 teaspoons baking powder

$^3/_8$ teaspoon salt

8 tablespoons (1 stick) unsalted butter

$^3/_4$ cup maple sugar or organic light or dark brown sugar

$^3/_4$ cup dark (grade B) maple syrup

$1^1/_2$ teaspoons vanilla extract

3 eggs, at room temperature

1 cup mashed cooked winter squash, such as kabocha, Perfection, or butternut

$1^1/_2$ cups (about 16) Medjool dates, pitted and quartered

1. Preheat the oven to 350°F. Generously butter and flour a 9-inch springform pan. Combine the flour, baking powder, and salt in a bowl and stir them together with a whisk to blend.

2. Cream the butter with the sugar in the bowl of an electric mixer on high speed until light and fluffy, 3 to 4 minutes. Lower the speed and slowly pour the syrup into the butter mixture. Add the vanilla and then the eggs, one at a time, beating until each one is well incorporated, scraping down the bowl between additions. When well blended, stir in the squash.

3. With the mixer on low speed, add the flour mixture in ½-cup increments until all is incorporated. Remove the mixing bowl and, using a large rubber scraper, give the batter several turns, scraping along the sides and bottom of the bowl to make sure all the flour has been incorporated. Finally, add the dates to the batter. Scrape the batter into the pan and even out the surface.

4. Bake in the center of the oven until firm and springy and a cake tester comes out clean, 60 to 70 minutes. When mostly cool, release the rim and carefully transfer the cake from the pan to a cake plate. Serve slightly warm or at room temperature, plain or with an accompaniment.

WINTER SQUASH SPICE CAKE

Add to the dry ingredients 1 teaspoon ground cinnamon, ½ teaspoon freshly grated nutmeg, ½ teaspoon ground allspice, and ⅛ teaspoon ground cloves.

Chocolate Bark with Cardamom and Sea Salt, Apricots, and Pistachios MAKES ONE 10 x 6-INCH SLAB

SHARDS OF BROKEN bark put on the table with a bowl of tangerines, a plate of dates, some nuts to crack, or a few cookies make a winning dessert that can be put together with ease night after night if need be. A variety of spices, nuts, and fruits can go into chocolate bark—candied ginger, tangerine zest, diced prunes, apricots, toasted pecans and almonds, salted cashews, black pepper, anise seed, or cinnamon, to name but a few.

We now know that a bit of salt makes all the sweet things—like chocolate and caramel and even fruit—dance! You don't need measurements, as you'll see the first time you make bark. The chocolate I buy happens to come in 6-ounce blocks, so I use that. I also use chocolate that's in the 70% cacao range, but it needn't be exactly that, of course.

4 ounces (more or less) dark chocolate, chopped into chunks
$^1/_2$ teaspoon cardamom seeds, toasted in a dry skillet until fragrant
3 tablespoons Red Flame raisins and/or dried apricots, cut into small pieces
2 to 3 tablespoons salted green pistachio nuts, some left whole, some cut into large pieces
Maldon sea salt or other flaky salt

1. Line a large flat dish or baking sheet with a piece of aluminum foil or parchment about 10 x 8 inches.

2. Put the chocolate in a bowl and set it over a pan of simmering water with the cardamom seeds. When the chocolate has melted, stir in half the fruit and pistachios. Spread the mixture over the foil in a thin sheet, then press the remaining fruits and nuts lightly into the warm chocolate. Sprinkle lightly with the salt.

3. Refrigerate until the chocolate is well set, at least an hour. To serve, break the bark into pieces and pile them on a small plate or dish. Store any extra bark in a covered container or a wax paper bag and refrigerate. It will keep well for a few weeks—theoretically.

White Chocolate and Coconut Bark

with Lavender and Tangerine Zest MAKES ONE 10 x 8-INCH SLAB

MY SISTER CAME up with this one Christmas. It's one of the prettiest barks you can imagine, and if you love the flavors of coconut and orange, you'll be very happy indeed. I can't resist adding a few green pistachio nuts. I use salted ones—both because the salt adds to the flavor and because they tend to have the best color and texture.

Two 3¹/2-ounce bars Lindt white chocolate with coconut
1 to 2 tablespoons salted pistachio nuts, as green as possible, finely chopped
1 scant teaspoon lavender blossoms or dried rose petals
Tangerine zest removed with a citrus zester in long, thin pieces

1. Lay a piece of aluminum foil or parchment on a tray, about 8 x 10 inches. Melt the chocolate in a bowl set over barely simmering water. Keep the heat low and take care not to let the edges burn by scraping down the chocolate as it melts.

2. Spread the melted chocolate thinly over the foil. Sprinkle the nuts, lavender, and zest over the chocolate and lightly press them in. Refrigerate until set. Break into pieces and store in an airtight container set in a cool place or in a wax paper bag in the refrigerator, where it will keep for weeks.

Black Walnut Brown Sugar Cookies

ALTHOUGH BLACK WALNUTS thrive just about everywhere, the Midwest is where you're likely to find hulled meats. You can also order them over the Internet. When you get them, be sure to keep them in the freezer, for they are very oily and contact with air does not benefit them. Brown sugar and coffee are a good match for black walnuts. In fact, these crisp cookies, which keep for weeks in a covered container, are great for dunking into coffee—the heat brings out their flavor.

8 tablespoons (1 stick) unsalted butter
1 cup muscovado or organic light or dark brown sugar
1 tablespoon finely ground espresso beans
1 large egg
1¼ cups all-purpose flour
¼ teaspoon baking soda
¼ teaspoon salt
1 cup black walnut pieces

1. Preheat the oven to 350°F and lightly grease 2 sheet pans.

2. Cream the butter with the sugar and espresso in the bowl of an electric mixer on high speed until light and smooth, then add the egg and continue beating until incorporated. Stir in the flour, baking soda, and salt and then the walnuts.

3. Drop the dough onto the prepared pans by the heaping teaspoonful, leaving about 1½ inches between each one. Bake until lightly browned around the edges, about 10 minutes, then transfer to a rack. They'll be soft and chewy at first and then crisp as they cool.

Hazelnut–Chocolate Chunk Cookies

MAKES ABOUT FORTY 1$\frac{1}{2}$-INCH COOKIES

THE COMBINATION OF hazelnuts and chocolate in this round, domed cookie is especially good with pear and persimmon desserts, but in the end it's a really good chocolate chip cookie. I use a nutty hazelnut oil to replace some of the butter, but if you haven't any, use all butter.

$\frac{3}{4}$ cup hazelnuts

5 tablespoons unsalted butter

3 tablespoons hazelnut oil

$\frac{1}{3}$ cup organic brown sugar

$\frac{1}{2}$ cup organic white sugar

1 egg

$\frac{1}{2}$ teaspoon vanilla extract

1$\frac{1}{4}$ cups all-purpose flour or mixed all-purpose and whole wheat pastry flour

1 teaspoon baking powder

$\frac{1}{4}$ teaspoon salt

$\frac{2}{3}$ cup chopped dark chocolate

Confectioners' sugar for dusting (optional)

1. Preheat the oven to 350°F. Put the hazelnuts on an unlined sheet pan and toast them until they smell fragrant and their skins start to loosen, about 10 minutes. Let them cool briefly, then rub the nuts together in a towel to loosen the skins. Don't worry about some of them sticking.

2. Line a sheet pan with parchment. Grind ½ cup of the nuts in a hand grinder to produce a fine, flourlike meal. (Lacking a grinder that will do this, process them with the flour, baking powder, and salt in a food processor, although they won't be as fine.) Roughly chop the remaining ¼ cup and set aside.

3. Cream the butter, oil, and sugars until light and smooth. Beat in the egg and vanilla, again until smooth. Add the ground hazelnuts, flour, baking powder, and salt, then stir in the chopped nuts and chocolate.

4. Form the dough into balls the size of large hazelnuts. Place them a few inches apart on the parchment-lined sheet pan and bake until pale gold, about 15 minutes. Serve plain or dusted with confectioners' sugar. Cool on the pan, then store in a covered container or freeze.

CHAPTER 8

· Puddings and Gelées ·

This chapter is dedicated to soft, soothing desserts, but this isn't to say they can't also be lively. There's nothing timid about the tangy Butterscotch Pudding (page 188) or a Souffléed Pancake with Caramelized Apples and Aged Cheddar (page 196).

These desserts relate to fruit in different ways. Some are based on a fruit, others want fruits as garnishes and accompaniments, and a few leave all but dried fruits behind in favor of grains, as in the Indian Pudding (page 176) and Native Wild Rice Pudding (page 179). Actually, almost any grain can be turned into a pudding-like dessert. Rice, bulgur, farro, oats, and other grains have long been used in traditional desserts as well as in savory dishes—most consisting of the grain plus dried fruits, a sweetener, and some sort of dairy. Quinoa makes a fast little nutritious dessert that's free of the gluten that's so troubling to some.

While we tend to think of farmers' markets as places for produce, grains show up occasionally as well. I've encountered quinoa in Colorado, a lovely organic brown rice in California, cornmeal and rye in Iowa, native wild rice in Minnesota, and polenta and old strains of popcorn in Oregon. The flavor of fresh grains is especially full and sweet. The arresting aroma of freshly ground cornmeal will take you by surprise, and the taste and texture of the parched native wild rice is nothing like that of the cultivated paddy rice from California.

For setting jellylike desserts, strict vegetarians will want to use agar-agar, but I have chosen gelatin, because I prefer the consistent softness in the set that I can't get with agar-agar. I often make these desserts for myself when I want something sweet after a meal but nothing too caloric. Allowed to set in juice glasses, they offer a pretty, simple ending to a meal.

Finally, because fruit has such a strong affinity for cream in its various forms, I've included some fruit desserts that are very nearly as simple as putting them out with a pitcher of cream. Not only strawberries and peaches, but fruits you might not think of, such as persimmons and mulberries, are good with cream—in truth, most other fruits are—and bringing the two together makes that much more of a dessert.

Indian Pudding SERVES 8

INDIAN MEAL WAS once the name for corn, and Indian pudding is cornmeal cooked in milk, sweetened with molasses, seasoned with spices, and baked until glossy and brown. It's comforting and simple and oddly reminiscent of persimmon pudding. I can't imagine why it doesn't appear on every Thanksgiving table, except that it does tie up the oven for a few hours and really must be eaten while warm.

You might use a sweetener from your region, which could be molasses or sorghum or maple syrup—all of which show up at farmers' markets. But molasses is traditional.

This recipe is easy to cut in half. Eggs are sometimes included and sometimes not. Leave them out if you wish.

1 quart milk
^{1}/2 cup coarse yellow cornmeal
1 teaspoon salt
4 tablespoons (^{1}/2 stick) unsalted butter
^{1}/2 cup molasses, sorghum, or maple syrup
2 tablespoons all-purpose flour
2 tablespoons organic white or brown sugar
2 eggs, beaten (optional)
^{1}/2 teaspoon ground ginger
1 teaspoon ground cinnamon
^{1}/2 teaspoon ground or freshly grated nutmeg

1. Preheat the oven to 275°F. Butter a 2-quart gratin dish. Bring 3 cups of the milk to a boil. Gradually whisk in the cornmeal and salt and cook over low heat, stirring constantly, until creamy, 10 to 15 minutes. Remove from the heat and stir in the butter and molasses.

3. Mix the flour and sugar together in a bowl and then add the eggs, if using. Whisk in a little of the hot cornmeal to temper the eggs, then whisk them back into the rest. Add the spices. Scrape the batter into the baking dish and pour over the rest of the milk. Bake until the pudding is very brown and glossy, about 2¼ hours. It will set sooner but gets better if you let it go the full time.

4. Let cool for 30 minutes before serving. It will still be warm and ready for cold cream or a scoop of vanilla ice cream.

Quinoa Pudding with Dried Cherries and Cranberries

MAKES ABOUT 2 1/2 CUPS

THIS IS A little like the impromptu dessert we had when we were kids—an extra portion of rice with a pat of butter, brown sugar, and cinnamon, and milk poured over all. It's that easy to make, only it's better. And it makes a good breakfast cereal, too.

Because quinoa lacks gluten it doesn't make a creamy pudding like rice does. Rather, it makes a dish that's mild, crunchy, and sustaining with distinct grains.

White quinoa is most common, but there are also red and black varieties. I buy the red variety at my local co-op and use it with the white. If it's not available, use all white.

2/3 cup white quinoa

1/3 cup red quinoa

3/8 teaspoon salt

1 tablespoon unsalted butter or more, to taste

2 tablespoons honey or agave nectar, to taste

3 tablespoons dried cranberries

2 tablespoons dried cherries, sweet or sour

Milk or cream

Ground cinnamon

1/4 cup toasted slivered almonds or chopped pecans

1. Rinse the quinoa in a sieve to wash off any saponin, the natural bitter coating that protects the grain from marauding birds. Most of it will have been removed already, but it doesn't hurt to rinse it again.

2. Bring 2 cups of water to a boil, then add the salt and quinoa. Reduce the heat to a simmer, cover the pan, and cook for 20 minutes, or until the germ is visible. Even when done, quinoa should have a little crunch. If the quinoa hasn't absorbed all of the water, drain it, and then return the quinoa to the pan. Stir in the butter and honey to taste and scatter the dried fruits over the top. Cover until the fruits are soft and plump, about 5 minutes.

3. Serve the quinoa in shallow bowls with a little milk or cream around it, dusted with cinnamon and sprinkled with the toasted nuts.

Native Wild Rice Pudding
with Maple Syrup and Wine-Soaked Cherries SERVES 6 to 8

HAND-GATHERED NATIVE WILD rice is quite different from the cultivated variety sold as "wild rice." The grains are soft gray-green and brown and of moderate length rather than long, shiny, and black, and it cooks more quickly, too. You can find real wild rice at Minnesota farmers' markets and over the Internet.

This earthy-watery grain of the North requires its regional counterparts—maple syrup and maple sugar for sweetening, and a spoonful of the Dried (most likely Michigan) Cherries in Red Wine. As wild rice has no gluten, you have to cook it with white rice to get a creamy texture. This recipe is based on one of Lucia Watson's, a heartland chef of distinction. Using a double boiler means you can leave the rice pretty much unattended for an hour or more.

3 cups milk
$1/3$ cup white rice
$1/3$ cup native wild rice
$1/4$ teaspoon salt
2 tablespoons unsalted butter, plus extra for the dish
2 or 3 egg yolks
$1/3$ cup plus maple sugar or organic light brown sugar
$1/3$ cup maple syrup
$1/2$ cup milk or cream
Dried Cherries in Red Wine (page 266)
Heavy cream for serving

1. Heat water in the bottom of a double boiler. Warm the milk in the top part over a separate burner. Add the two rices, salt, and butter, and set the mixture over the now simmering water. Cover and cook until the milk is absorbed, about $1\frac{1}{4}$ hours. Check the pot after 30 minutes to make sure there's plenty of water; add more if needed.

2. Preheat the oven to 325°F and butter a 6- to 8-cup baking dish.

3. Whisk the egg yolks with $\frac{1}{4}$ cup of the sugar, the maple syrup, and the milk or cream. Gently stir this into the warm rice. Add all to the buttered dish, shake to distribute the contents, and sprinkle the remaining tablespoon of sugar over the top. Bake until the rice is set and the surface is handsomely burnished, 30 to 40 minutes. Serve warm with the cherries and cold cream.

Honeyed Semolina Pudding with Wine Syrup

SERVES 8

THIS COOL, DENSE pudding tasting of honey and wine can be a summer or a winter dessert, though in summer you might forgo the syrup in favor of a fresh sauce made from berries—with some berries on the side. Dried or fresh fruits poached in wine or syrup are a good match with this dessert.

You can serve this pudding from the dish, scooping out attractive oval mounds, but it's firm enough that you can also put it into an attractive mold, something that makes a more formal presentation. There will be 3 cups of pudding, so choose a mold that will hold 3 to 4 cups. A narrow bread pan will give you a loaf to slice. However you slice it—in wedges or slabs—drizzle the wine syrup over the top just before serving.

THE PUDDING

One $1/4$-ounce envelope unflavored gelatin
2 cups milk
$1/4$ teaspoon salt
Scant $1/2$ cup honey
$1/2$ cup semolina
2 tablespoons Marsala or port
1 cup heavy cream

THE WINE SYRUP

$1^1/2$ cups Marsala, port, Pedro Ximénez, or red wine
$1/2$ cup organic sugar
One 2-inch piece vanilla bean, halved lengthwise
$1/2$ teaspoon peppercorns, toasted in a skillet until fragrant
One 1-inch piece cinnamon stick
1 large piece orange zest removed with a vegetable peeler

1. Sprinkle the gelatin over $1/4$ cup water in a small bowl and set aside to soften.

2. Heat the milk with the salt and the honey in a saucepan over medium-low heat, stirring to dissolve the honey. Whisk in the semolina. Continue to stir for a few minutes, until the semolina has thickened. Remove from the heat and stir in the softened gelatin followed by the wine. Let cool, but occasionally give it a stir to keep the temperature even. You want it to fall nearly to room temperature—not so warm as to melt the cream, but not so cool that the gelatin starts to set.

3. Whip the cream until fairly stiff. Fold it into the cooled semolina, leaving it streaky, then scrape the mixture into a waiting bowl or mold. Refrigerate for a few hours, until set. To unmold, dip the dish into very hot water and hold until it begins to loosen, then set a plate over the top and invert.

4. To make the wine syrup, put all the ingredients in a small saucepan and bring to a boil. Cook at a slow boil until the surface is covered with bubbles and about $\frac{1}{3}$ cup remains. Serve warm or at room temperature. (Store any leftover syrup in the refrigerator, where it will keep indefinitely.)

I have noticed that raw honey sometimes makes the milk curdle. Honey experts have been at something of a loss to explain why this is so but suggest that heating the milk and honey slowly can prevent curdling. If curdling does happen, simply strain the milk and discard the clumps.

Coconut Rice Pudding Cake SERVES 8 OR MORE

To GET THE flavor of coconut, you have to use two cans of coconut milk—it's just a bit too subtle with only one. For rice, I use a medium-grain white rice, not as easy to source as it once was, but you can find it at Asian markets. Look for Hime's organically grown premium medium white rice, or Tamaki Gold, both grown in California. I've also used risotto rice on occasion although it's shorter and starchier.

Serve this with fresh pineapple and cream, a succulent dice of ripe honeydew melon with slivers of fresh mint, or fresh or canned lychees.

1 cup medium-grain white rice
$3/8$ teaspoon salt
Two 14-ounce cans coconut milk, plus milk or water to make
    4 cups
$1/2$ cup plus 2 tablespoons organic white or light brown sugar
One 2-inch piece vanilla bean, halved lengthwise,
    or $1^1/2$ teaspoons vanilla extract
3 eggs

1. Briefly rinse the rice in a bowl of water (it need not run clear), then put it in a pan with $1^3/4$ cups water and the salt. Bring to a boil, lower the heat, cover the pan, and simmer until the water is absorbed, about 15 minutes.

2. Pour the coconut milk into a 4-cup measure and add milk or water to make 4 cups. Heat it in a saucepan with the sugar and vanilla bean, then add the rice. Simmer, stirring occasionally, until thick but a creamy layer of liquid remains on top, about 30 minutes. Preheat the oven to 350°F.

3. Select an 8- or 9-inch springform pan or bread pan that will hold 6 cups of liquid. Line the bottom with foil or parchment paper, using enough to just reach over the seam in the springform pan so that no leakage occurs. Butter the sides and bottom generously with soft butter.

4. Whisk the eggs with the vanilla extract, if using. Whisk in a cup of the rice to temper the eggs, then add the rest and combine well. Pour the rice mixture into the prepared baking pan, set it on a sheet pan, and bake until pulling away from the edges and a knife inserted in the center comes out clean, 50 to 55 minutes.

5. Slide a knife around the edge of the pan, let the pudding settle for at least 15 minutes or until cool, and then turn it onto a plate. Peel away the paper. Slice and serve warm or cold.

VEGAN VARIATION

For a vegan rice pudding, use coconut milk mixed with soy milk or water, cook it on the stove until more of the liquid is absorbed, and don't bake it, thus eliminating the eggs.

RICE PUDDING CAKE WITH LEMON AND CINNAMON

Use regular milk instead of coconut milk. Once the rice is cooked, add the finely grated zest of 2 large lemons and ¼ teaspoon ground cinnamon. For a winter dessert, serve with chilled cream and a spoonful of any of the poached dried fruits, such as the Figs in Pedro Ximénez (page 148), Prunes Simmered in Red Wine (page 147), or either of the small dried fruit in wine (page 267 or 269).

Sweet Potato–Coconut Pudding

with Toasted Coconut SERVES 6 TO 8

TRUE, SWEET POTATOES aren't fruit, but they make a great pudding. Dark muscovado sugar has a molasses note that's just right with the sweet potato and the coconut milk.

For sweet potatoes, use the orange-fleshed varieties, like Jewel and Garnet. Yes, they're called yams, but they really are sweet potatoes.

Serve at room temperature with whipped cream and golden coconut strips, or warm, with cold cream.

2 cups cooked sweet potatoes (1$\frac{1}{2}$ pounds sweet potatoes)
One 14-ounce can coconut milk (1$\frac{3}{4}$ cups)
2 teaspoons vanilla extract
3 eggs
$\frac{7}{8}$ cup dark muscovado sugar or organic dark brown sugar
$\frac{1}{4}$ teaspoon salt
$\frac{1}{2}$ pint softly whipped cream flavored with rum, to taste
$\frac{1}{2}$ cup wide strips dried coconut

1. If you don't have sweet potatoes already cooked, chop them into large pieces and steam until tender, about 30 minutes. Peel, then coarsely mash. Preheat the oven to 350°F. Put a kettle of water on to boil for the water bath.

2. Puree the cooked sweet potato flesh in a blender or food processor with the remaining ingredients, except the whipped cream and coconut, until smooth.

3. Pour the pudding mixture into a 2 quart baking dish. Set it in a larger dish and add the boiling water to come halfway up the sides. Bake until the pudding is firm, 45 to 50 minutes. Before the oven cools, toast the coconut shavings on a sheet pan until crisp and golden, just a few minutes.

4. Once the pudding has cooled, whip the cream and flavor it with rum. Mound the cream over the pudding, cover with the toasted coconut, and serve.

Dark Chocolate Pudding MAKES 2 CUPS, SERVING 4 TO 6

WHEN IT COMES to cocoa, I'm partial to Penzeys. They claim that it's twice as rich as other cocoas, and I'm inclined to agree that it is. Chocolate pudding is delicious with cold cream, but for fruit, consider sugared blackberries, Strawberries in Red Wine Syrup (page 64), or Dried Cherries in Red Wine (page 266).

2 cups milk

1 teaspoon finely grated orange zest

1 ounce dark chocolate, 60% to 70% cacao

1/2 cup unsweetened cocoa powder, plus extra for dusting

1/2 cup organic sugar

1/4 teaspoon salt

1/4 cup cornstarch dissolved in 1/4 cup milk or water

1/4 teaspoon almond extract

5 tablespoons cold cream

1. Warm half the milk with the orange zest and dark chocolate in a saucepan over low heat. Meanwhile, combine the cocoa, sugar, and salt in a bowl. Stir in 1/3 cup water to make a smooth paste. Whisk the paste into the warm milk.

2. Mix the cornstarch with the remaining milk, then add it to the saucepan.

3. Raise the heat to medium-high and cook, stirring constantly, until the mixture thickens. Then lower the heat and cook, stirring, for a few minutes more. Remove from the heat and immediately stir in the almond extract.

4. Pour the pudding into 4 to 6 small bowls, ramekins, or cups. Press plastic wrap directly onto the surface to keep a skin from forming, or leave it off if you don't mind it. Serve chilled with cream poured over the top and a dusting of cocoa.

186 SEASONAL FRUIT DESSERTS

Butterscotch Pudding with Sweet and Savory Pecans

SERVES 4 TO 6

TWO LITTLE CHANGES to an old standard—using the molasses-saturated dark brown muscovado sugar in place of regular brown sugar and crème fraîche in place of cream—yield a butterscotch pudding that hits home with intensity and zing. I serve these puddings with toasted pecans glazed with melted sugar along with a pinch of salt and some pepper.

A wide saucepan with low sides rather than a small one with high sides cooks everything more evenly. If your sugar is rock-hard and you don't have time to soften it, estimate the amount and know that it will dissolve in the hot milk.

THE PUDDING

1 cup whole or 2% milk
1/2 cup dark muscovado sugar
1 cup crème fraîche or whole-milk yogurt
1/4 teaspoon salt
3 tablespoons cornstarch or arrowroot dissolved in
    3 tablespoons cold water
1 teaspoon vanilla extract
3 tablespoons unsalted butter

TO FINISH

1/4 cup pecans
1 teaspoon unsalted butter
1 tablespoon organic sugar
Salt and freshly ground pepper

1. Warm the milk with the sugar in a saucepan over low heat, stirring until the sugar is completely dissolved. Add the crème fraîche, salt, and dissolved cornstarch. Turn the heat up to medium and cook, stirring constantly with a wooden spoon, until the pudding begins to clump up and thicken on the bottom, after 4 or 5 minutes. Switch to a whisk and whisk briskly until the pudding has thickened, then cook for at least 1 minute more to get rid of the raw cornstarch taste. Remove from the heat and whisk in the vanilla and butter.

2. Pour the pudding into individual cups or glasses and refrigerate until cool.

3. Toast the pecans in a toaster oven set at 300°F until they begin to smell fragrant, after 5 minutes or so. Melt the butter in a small skillet over medium heat. Add the pecans, sprinkle the sugar over them, and cook, stirring more or less constantly, until the sugar has melted and has begun to coat the nuts with caramel, 3 or 4 minutes. Remove and sprinkle with salt and a little freshly ground pepper. Let cool to harden.

4. Chop the pecans, coarsely or finely, as you wish. Sprinkle a thick layer over the pudding just before serving.

Tangelo-Tangerine Pudding MAKES FOUR $\frac{1}{2}$-CUP SERVINGS

THIS ELECTRIC ORANGE pudding is great for someone who's longing for dessert but trying to say no. Tangelos are big and juicy with a decidedly round and sparkly flavor, but any tangerine-type citrus at its sweet prime will be a good bet. A mixture of citrus—grapefruits, tangerines, blood oranges, a bit of lime—is also intriguing, a kind of tutti-frutti. Or use just blood orange juice, if you can find it.

If you choose to use bottled juice, look for one that is freshly squeezed, if possible. I have occasionally found some fine juices at farmers' markets and farm stands where citrus are plentiful.

1 heaping teaspoon finely grated tangerine, tangelo, or other citrus zest
1 tablespoon organic sugar
3 tablespoons organic cornstarch
2 cups fresh tangelo juice (from 10 to 12 tangelos) or mixed citrus juice
Tiny pinch of salt
1 tablespoon unsalted butter
1 teaspoon bottled yuzu juice or 1 tablespoon orange-flower water
Stevia, orange blossom honey, or agave nectar, to taste

1. Smash the tangerine zest with the sugar to moisten the sugar with the fruit's aromatic oils. Transfer to a 1-quart saucepan along with the cornstarch, juice, and salt. Stir to dissolve the cornstarch.

2. Turn on the heat, bring the mixture to a boil, and cook, stirring, until the juice has thickened, after just a few minutes. Cook for 1 minute more, then turn off the heat and whisk in the butter and yuzu or orange-flower water. Taste, and if extra sweetener is needed, add a few drops of stevia, orange blossom honey, or agave nectar.

3. Divide among juice glasses or Champagne glasses. Refrigerate until set, about 2 hours. (If you're not counting calories too carefully, this pudding is great with a dollop of whipped cream.)

CITRUS ARE PROMISCUOUS. They interbreed with ease and produce variations seemingly without end, which makes keeping up with new varieties something of a challenge. I am not going to attempt to explain who's who in terms of lineage and bloodlines here, but just point out a few named fruits to look for.

In general, you can think of tangerines as those smallish citrus that are easy to peel and whose segments are easily separated. Like any citrus, if they've been picked early in their season, they can be tart. There are some years when tangerines, Clementines, Mandarins, and oranges are all astonishingly sweet—usually the first year of drought when sugars are concentrated but the trees aren't yet too stressed. And there are years when, due to other conditions, they remain tart throughout the season. Although people quickly put citrus together with Florida, in fact they grow well in Texas, Arizona, and California, including in the Sierra foothills of central California, for there are varieties that can take the chill of higher elevations.

The season begins with Satsumas, a large class of Mandarins that came to California from Japan in the 1870s. They are so filled with vitamin C and other nutrients that many vouch for their ability to prevent colds. Each November we receive a box from California, and since we have no place to keep twenty-five pounds of fruit, we eat many Satsumas each day. Neither my husband nor I has had a cold in about ten years, and I'm sure this is why. In 2008 Dr. Andrew Breksa of the USDA noted that ten ounces of Placer County Satsuma Mandarin juice contains as much synephrine as a Sudafed decongestant tablet. Health claims aside, they are refreshing and good to eat out of hand, and they make wonderful juice and geleés, too.

The season ends with a tiny tangerine called the Pixie. Grown mainly in Ojai, California, the Pixie was developed comparatively recently, in 1965. This late spring fruit is seedless, has copious amounts of juice, and is sweeter than all the other Mandarins. Once the Pixies have entered the market, you know it's time to say good-bye to fresh citrus (there will still be some in storage) and start looking toward rhubarb and the first strawberries.

In between November and April a parade of citrus marches to market—Dancy (arriving around Christmas), Page (with thick, deep orange skin), the big juicy Honeybells (Mandarin-orange hybrids with a little knob on one end), loose-skinned Clementines with their reddish-orange skin, the small spherical Fairchilds, the slightly larger oblate Murcotts, or honey tangerines, and more. This display of diversity is one of the pleasures of winter fruit.

Also on the small side are limequats, or calamondin, and kumquats, whose skins are sweet and insides sour, the ultimate sweet-tart if you take a big bite of both skin and flesh. The acidic calamondin juice makes a great marinade and seasoning for fish and lends a sharp accent to overly sweet tangerine juice.

One especially exotic citrus to look for is a kind of citron called Buddha's Hand. Its long fingerlike appendages are all skin, pith, and perfume. Its zest can be used as flavoring and the whole thing used for candying, but I just put one out where I can see it and inhale its sweet fragrance.

Bergamot orange is another floral citrus. Its zest is the flavoring in Earl Grey tea, but its tart juice and aromatic zest can go into sorbets, geleés, and even marmalades. They're rarely seen, but interesting to play with should you find them.

Native Persimmon Pudding SERVES 6

When considering America's native persimmon for Slow Food's Ark of Taste, a few of us tested its worth by making persimmon puddings using frozen wild persimmon pulp. The native fruit did make an exceptional pudding. I think the Hachiya compares quite favorably, especially by the time you've brought in the brown sugar and all. But the native is more complex, with almost tropical nuances.

This is a pudding, not a cake. It will be moist and soft. Persimmon puddings are always rich, and they always taste perfect with cream, with or without a shot of bourbon mixed in.

2 eggs, separated
1 cup organic light brown sugar
2 cups persimmon pulp, fresh or defrosted frozen, from native persimmons or ripe Hachiyas
6 tablespoons unsalted butter, melted
$2/3$ cup half-and-half
$1/3$ cup buttermilk or yogurt mixed with 1 teaspoon baking soda
1 cup all-purpose flour
$1/4$ teaspoon salt
$1^{1}/2$ teaspoons baking powder
$1/2$ teaspoon ground cinnamon

1. Preheat the oven to 325°F. Butter a soufflé dish or a gratin dish.

2. Beat the egg yolks, sugar, and persimmon pulp together in a bowl, then stir in the melted butter, half-and-half, and buttermilk mixture. In a second bowl, combine the flour, salt, baking powder, and cinnamon. Add the dry ingredients to the wet persimmon mixture, stirring slowly with a whisk to combine them well.

3. Whisk the egg whites until they are firm but not dry. Fold them into the batter and then turn everything into the prepared dish. Bake until the pudding has risen and is firm, about 45 minutes. The center will fall, but that's fine. Serve warm or at room temperature with cream—softly whipped cream or poured heavy cream.

persimmons

I GREW UP IN CALIFORNIA where we were familiar with the Asian Hachiyas and Fuyus, rather than the native variety that flourishes in the Midwest and South. I didn't have my first native persimmon until just a few years ago. I scooped one up off a lawn, picked off stray blades of grass, and popped it in my mouth. What a surprise! It was almost tropical in flavor, as if a little passion fruit or guava had slipped in. "Gorgeous!" said my mouth, but the fruit itself was wrinkled and the flesh was mushy—indeed, a mess. But that degree of ripeness is needed if the tannins are to be tamed and the fruit is to be edible. There are midwesterners who are so passionate about the native persimmon that they collect the pulp, separate it from its large seeds, then package it. A container of frozen native persimmon pulp makes the best persimmon pudding you've probably ever tasted, though there's nothing disappointing about one made from Hachiyas.

Like the native persimmon, the Hachiya type is extremely astringent until it's practically falling out of its skin, and then it's like eating silk. In California there are still traditional Japanese farmers who undertake the laborious process of drying (and massaging) Hachiya persimmons to make hoshigaki, a succulent, gorgeous morsel, which has been boarded by Slow Food Ark of Taste.

The flattish Fuyu type can be enjoyed while still crisp, though usually the skins are tough and best peeled. Eventually they soften too, and you can use the pulp to make a pudding. But as they don't yield a lot, you're better off buying two big Hachiyas and letting them ripen.

Souffléed Pancake with Caramelized Apples and Aged Cheddar SERVES 2 TO 4

THIS DINNER IN the form of dessert was often on our table during the chilly winter my husband and I spent on the west coast of Ireland. Heating the oven helped mitigate the damp cold of our cottage, as did the generous splash of Irish whiskey added to the apples and our glasses. We used big, tart Bramleys, which you won't find here, but look for Wolf River, Rhode Island Greening, Newtown Pippin, or Gravenstein. A sharp aged Cheddar goes quite nicely with the caramelized apples—sweet and salty tastes at once.

THE PANCAKE

2 tablespoons unsalted butter

3 tablespoons organic sugar

3 eggs

$^3/_4$ cup milk

$^1/_2$ teaspoon vanilla extract

$^1/_4$ teaspoon salt

$^1/_2$ cup all-purpose flour

THE APPLES

2 tablespoons unsalted butter

2 tablespoons organic white or light brown sugar

2 Wolf River or other tart apples, peeled, cored, and thinly sliced

2 tablespoons whiskey or bourbon

Aged Cheddar or aged Gouda cheese, thinly sliced

1. Preheat the oven to 425°F. Melt the butter in a 10-inch cast-iron skillet, brushing it once around the sides. Put the remaining pancake ingredients in a blender, add the melted butter, and blend until smooth, scraping down the sides once. Or mix everything together by hand. Let the batter rest while the oven heats.

2. Melt the butter for the apples in the same skillet, sprinkle on the sugar, and then add the apples. Cook over high heat, flipping them in the pan occasionally until they begin to caramelize, after several minutes. Lower the heat once the apple slices begin to color, turning them with increasing frequency until they're richly caramelized. Raise the heat, add the whiskey, and, being careful to stand back a bit, tilt the pan so that it will flame and burn off.

3. Pour the batter over the apples and bake until golden and puffed, 20 to 30 minutes. Serve immediately from the pan, with the cheese laid over the top.

Mocha Gelée MAKES FOUR ½-CUP SERVINGS

PERUVIAN CUSTARDS IN which milk is infused with coffee and vanilla beans are one of my favorite desserts, but they are a bit complicated to make and definitely rich. The same elements are brought together with a bit more ease in this gelée, which can be as rich or skinny as you wish.

1 cup milk
¼ cup heavy cream
1 cinnamon stick
One 1-inch piece vanilla bean, slit lengthwise, or
    ½ teaspoon vanilla extract
1½ ounces dark chocolate
¼ cup organic light brown sugar
One ¼-ounce envelope unflavored gelatin
1 cup brewed espresso or strong coffee
⅛ teaspoon almond extract
3 tablespoons cold cream
Unsweetened cocoa powder or ground cinnamon

1. Heat the milk and cream with the cinnamon stick, vanilla bean, if using, chocolate, and sugar. Stir to dissolve the sugar and melt the chocolate, then turn off the heat and steep for 15 minutes. If using a vanilla bean, be sure to scrape its seeds into the milk.

2. While the milk is steeping, soften the gelatin in ¼ cup cold water for 5 minutes. Add it to the hot milk and stir to dissolve, reheating the milk if it has become too cool to dissolve the gelatin easily.

3. Add the coffee to the pan along with the vanilla extract, if using, and the almond extract. Pour through a strainer into a liquid measuring cup, then pour into glasses or ramekins. Refrigerate until set and well chilled, about 4 hours.

4. Serve with a spoonful of cold cream poured over the top, and a dusting of cocoa or cinnamon.

Broken Jellied Wine with Summer Fruit SERVES 4 TO 6

WINE JELLY IS one of the prettiest, lightest, and easiest desserts you can make. After the wine has set, chop it into cubes and slivers so that the pieces sparkle. Then serve the broken jelly in wineglasses with summer fruit.

For the wine you can use Marsala, sherry, Riesling, or a sparkler like Champagne or Moscato di Asti. I'm especially fond of the latter. It's bubbly and aromatic, plus you'll have extra to pour over the jelly or drink alongside.

For fruit, choose those that are ripe and full of flavor—white peaches or nectarines, raspberries, or an aromatic melon. Slice those that need to be sliced into bite-sized pieces as close to serving as possible. Don't hesitate to mix fruits. White peaches and raspberries are always perfect together.

One 1/4-ounce envelope unflavored gelatin
1/3 cup organic sugar
1/2 cup wine or water
1 1/2 cups sweet and/or sparkling wine
2 tablespoons fresh lemon juice
1 to 1 1/2 cups fruit, cut or sliced into small pieces and lightly sugared

1. Sprinkle the gelatin over 1/4 cup cold water and set it aside to soften.

2. Combine the sugar with the 1/2 cup wine in a saucepan. Bring to a boil, then lower the heat and simmer, stirring occasionally, until the sugar is dissolved. Remove from the heat and stir in the softened gelatin. Stir until it's thoroughly dissolved, then pour it into the rest of the wine along with the lemon juice. Mix well, then pour into a bowl or a compote dish and refrigerate until set. Wine seems to take longer to set than cream or fruit juices, so plan on at least 6 hours, or even overnight for a firm set.

3. Chop the jelly into cubes, then serve it in the compote or in wine or Champagne glasses interspersed with the fruit.

Pomegranate Gelée

with Saffron-Yogurt Cream and Pistachios SERVES 4 TO 6

I DEVELOPED THIS recipe for an event that featured both pomegranate juice and pistachio nuts. This seemed like a good way to bring them together. Pure, unpasteurized pomegranate juice is an intense drink, so a little goes a long way. It also happens to be a powerful source of antioxidants.

I let the gelée firm up in small juice glasses, leaving enough room for the saffron-yogurt topping, inspired by an Indian dessert, *mishi doi*. This is a somewhat unusual dessert. If saffron and yogurt seem strange, you can always use plain yogurt in their place. But I encourage you to give it a try.

THE GELÉE

2 cups pure pomegranate juice, such as Pom
One 1/4-ounce envelope unflavored gelatin
1 tablespoon organic sugar
2 teaspoons orange-flower water

THE YOGURT SAUCE

1/2 cup Greek yogurt or thick whole-milk yogurt
1 tablespoon honey, or more to taste
2 tablespoons milk
Small pinch of saffron threads
2 tablespoons peeled green pistachio nuts, coarsely chopped
1 tablespoon pomegranate seeds

1. Pour 1/2 cup of the pomegranate juice into a bowl, sprinkle the gelatin on top, and let it stand for 5 minutes.

2. Meanwhile, heat half the remaining juice just to the boiling point. Add the sugar and the juice with the gelatin, and stir until the gelatin is dissolved. Gradually add the rest of the juice and the orange-flower water. Divide among 4 to 6 small glasses and refrigerate until set, allowing at least 6 hours.

3. Stir the yogurt and honey together. Heat the milk with the saffron threads, let cool, and then stir into the yogurt. Spoon the yogurt cream over each glass of pomegranate jelly. Garnish with the pistachio nuts and a few pomegranate seeds.

fruit and cream

Desperate for a suddenly needed dessert, I made a fool from what remained of a dish of Strawberries in Red Wine Syrup (page 64). The berries had lost their glow, but pureed and folded into whipped cream, the red wine syrup leaving a trail of ruby streaks, they may have surpassed their original form. I can't think of a fruit that isn't enhanced by the addition of cream. Even something as seemingly ordinary as applesauce becomes special when you pour on a spoonful of heavy cream.

Peaches and cream or strawberries (or any berries) and cream are classics. In general, I prefer to use less cream and more fruit (one part cream to two or more parts fruit) so that the fruit flavor stays bright and forward. Crème fraîche, or a sabayon to which whipped cream has been added, brings a little sharpness to fruit. And cream can even give way to a creamy yogurt when tartness—and fewer calories—are desired.

While a fool is meant to take center stage, garnished with a crisp little cookie, you might consider one as a sauce to serve with other fruits, such as the Blackberry Fool on page 206 over sliced peaches.

Strawberries with **Maple Sugar and Cream** SERVES 4 TO 6

ONE HARDLY NEEDS a recipe for a dish of strawberries and cream, but I do actually remember two aunts arguing over the best way to "make" this old-fashioned, best of desserts. Clearly people do have their preferences, especially about the simplest things. Should the cream be sweet or sour? If sweet, should it be whipped or poured? Do you mash some of the berries first to work up a little sauce or leave them utterly untouched? And what about adding a splash of Kirsch? These details I leave to you.

Pass a plate of cookies or serve with a slice of Yeasted Sugar Cake (page 242), which brings you pretty close to strawberry shortcake.

1 quart fragrant, ripe strawberries
$^1\!/_4$ cup maple sugar or organic light brown sugar, or to taste
1 tablespoon Kirsch, limoncello, or Cointreau, or more to taste
1 cup heavy cream, crème fraîche, or a combination

1. Quickly rinse the berries, then set them on a clean towel and blot dry. Remove the stems and the leaves with a paring knife or the tip of a vegetable peeler. Mash them with a potato masher, leaving quite a bit of texture. Stir the sugar into the fruit, add the Kirsch, cover, and refrigerate.

2. If using heavy cream, whip it until fairly stiff, then fold it into the mashed berries. Pile the mixture into a bowl or individual serving dishes. It can be refrigerated for 2 hours before serving. If using crème fraîche, whisk it so that it's smooth and thick, but not too much, then fold it into the fruit. A third alternative is to whip cream and crème fraîche together—that way you get the volume of the cream but a little tartness from the crème fraîche.

Blackberry Fool SERVES 4

THE BERRIES CAN be sugared
and refrigerated ahead of
time, the cream also whipped
and refrigerated, but the
two are best folded together
just before serving, as the
berries can be very juicy.

Blackberries with Rose Water (page 42)
$1/2$ cup heavy cream
$1/3$ cup crème fraîche
1 tablespoon confectioners' sugar

1. Crush about a quarter of the berries with a pestle, then
set them aside in the refrigerator to macerate for an hour if
time allows. If not, go ahead to the next step.

2. Whip the cream and crème fraîche with the confectioners'
sugar until stiff but not grainy.

3. If the berries have given up a lot of juice, pour it off into
a cup. Fold the cream and berries together using just a few
strokes, then serve in bowls or glasses. Pour the juice over
as a garnish.

Mulberries and Crème Fraîche SERVES 4

SINCE PUTTING DRIP irrigation around a number of once-mysterious trees growing in the back of my garden, I've discovered, to my delight, that one of them is a mulberry tree, which, for a brief time, puts out dark bullet-shaped fruits with a pebbly texture. They are not as big as the plump Persian kind, but they are quite usable.

Even though they vaguely resemble blackberries, mulberries have their own very unique musky flavor. Fragile and juicy, they stain like crazy, so if, at the farmers' market, a vendor pours them into a paper bag for you, find a plastic bag right away, or they will soon bleed through and stain whatever they touch, including your car seat.

2 cups mulberries
2 to 3 teaspoons organic light brown sugar or maple sugar, to taste
Rose water (optional)
1/2 cup crème fraîche

1. Look over the mulberries and remove any large stems. If the fruit is ripe and soft, you might decide to just leave tiny stems in place. Sprinkle with a few teaspoons of sugar, or more if the fruit is tart, then sprinkle on a few drops of rose water if desired.

2. Stir the crème fraîche with a fork to loosen it, then drizzle it over the berries and serve.

Persimmon Fool SERVES 4 OR MORE

PERSIMMON PULP ISN'T thick, so this fool probably won't be either. But it's cool and frothy and great with a Hazelnut–Chocolate Chunk Cookie (page 172) or Maple Sugar Shortbread (page 29) on the side.

2 very ripe Hachiya persimmons
Organic brown sugar
1/4 teaspoon ground cinnamon
1/8 teaspoon freshly grated nutmeg
1/2 cup heavy cream
1/2 cup crème fraîche
2 tablespoons chopped toasted pecans or hazelnuts

1. Scoop the flesh out of the persimmon skins. You should have about 2 cups or a little less. Break it up with a fork so that it's fairly smooth. Taste, and if it needs sweetening, add a little sugar. You probably won't need more than a few teaspoons, if that. Season with the cinnamon and nutmeg.

2. Whip the cream and crème fraîche together until fairly stiff but not grainy.

3. Fold the cream into the persimmon puree, leaving it streaky, and then spoon it into dessert glasses. Garnish with the chopped nuts and serve.

VARIATION
Freeze in an ice cream maker to make a soft ice cream and serve it within a few hours, before it hardens, as there is not enough sugar here to give it a real ice cream texture.

Rhubarb Fool SERVES 8 TO 10

ONE RECIPE OF the cooked rhubarb on page 79 will yield enough fool for 8 to 10 servings, more than you might want, so feel free to use less and make less. My rule of thumb is to use half as much cream as fruit (or less) so that you can really taste the fruit.

3 cups Green or Red Rhubarb Puree (page 79), well chilled
1 cup heavy cream
Confectioners' sugar
¼ cup or more Rhubarb Syrup (page 73; optional)

1. Taste the rhubarb to determine how tart it is.

2. Whip the cream with confectioners' sugar to taste, adding more than you normally would to make up for the tartness of the fruit. It should be a little firmer than cream you'd use for a garnish, but not so firm that it becomes grainy.

3. Fold the cream and rhubarb together, leaving the mixture streaky. Then fold in the syrup if using. Mound into bowls or glasses and serve.

Peaches and Raspberries
Layered with Honey Sabayon SERVES 6

You CAN GILD the lily of this coupe by drizzling Blackcap Raspberry Sauce over the peaches and berries and sabayon. It's over the top—and worth it! Make the sabayon earlier in the day, fold in the whipped cream an hour or two ahead of time, and slice the peaches before you sit down. Then it's just a matter of putting all the parts together.

3 egg yolks, preferably organic
2 tablespoons mild honey
1/3 cup Marsala or Moscato di Asti
1/2 cup heavy cream
6 ripe peaches or nectarines, white or yellow
1 or 2 handfuls of raspberries or blackberries
1/4 cup Blackcap Raspberry Sauce (page 256)

1. Break the yolks into a bowl that will sit over, but not in, a pan of simmering water. (If it's touching, you'll end up with scrambled eggs.) Whisk in the honey and the wine, then set the bowl over the simmering water and whisk constantly until the sauce is thick and foamy and no clear liquid remains in the bowl when you pull away the foam. If you see any egg mixture that hasn't been incorporated, keep whisking. In all this will take about 5 minutes. Refrigerate immediately.

2. Once the sabayon is cold, whip the cream into peaks just slightly firmer than usual, then fold it into the sabayon, leaving it a little streaky. Refrigerate until needed.

3. Dip the peaches into a pot of boiling water for 5 to 10 seconds. Immediately transfer them to a bowl of ice water and then slip off the skins. Slice the peaches into a bowl. To serve, make layers of peaches, berries, and sabayon in glasses or in a compote. Drizzle the berry sauce over the sabayon as you go, then serve.

CHAPTER 9

• Cheese and Dairy Desserts •

While the focus of this book has been on fruits and fruit desserts, cheese and other dairy go so well with fruits, fresh and dried, that they can't be left out. Our new American cheeses represent regionalism, craft, and the kind of small-scale production that puts them on the same level as heirloom fruits.

Dairy desserts can be many things, but I've limited this selection to those sweets that take especially well to fruits. You'll find custard, Swedish creams based on cultured dairy, a few mousses, two tarts, and one ice cream along with cheeses paired with fruits. I think you'll find that these desserts can be used in a variety of ways, with fruit or without.

Sometimes a light dairy dessert is truly appealing, and you can easily make the adjustments you need by choosing the dairy you prefer. When I go with the richer options, which I'll do for a special meal, I make smaller servings, a compromise I'm happy with. But whether you prefer full fat or something else, I think it's important to buy organic products, especially butter and cream, since traces of pesticides tend to reside in the fat.

Dairy might not be dairy at all, but dairylike—such as those desserts made from soy milk or coconut cream, nut milks, and the like. I often use soy milk but am not a huge fan of nut milks, unless they're homemade, and then they can be superb—but expensive.

Regardless of your preferences, all dairy desserts go well with fruit, from simple macerated fruits to fruit sauces and purees and wine-preserved compotes. And pies and crisps practically beg for a scoop of ice cream, honey mousse, or whipped cream or chilled cream to which nothing has been done. Even just a little—a few teaspoons of cream—pulls the diverse flavors of a baked fruit dessert together and makes them smoother and more flavorful than they were before.

Many interesting commercial ice creams are available today. Even in my country store I can count on finding cinnamon ice cream, lemon verbena, and many of the once oddball flavors I used to make myself, such as garam masala ice cream. In the interest of time and the wish to support the local artisans who make these ice creams, I am happy to buy them, and that is why I have included only the Yogurt-Honey Ice Cream in this collection. It's made quickly and easily, for no custard is involved, and it's as good with as many desserts as classic French vanilla. In fact, it has become my "vanilla" ice cream.

Swedish Cream with **Buttermilk** SERVES 6

CULTURED BUTTERMILK (and kefir) are low-fat, but full-bodied and tangy. You don't want to heat either directly, though, as they curdle, so take away the chill by setting the buttermilk over the hot cream while it steeps with the vanilla.

You can improvise with this dessert, replacing half the buttermilk with the Apricot Sauce with Cardamom (page 254) or any of the other fruit purees in Chapter 11, except blueberries or blackberries, because the color will be odd. (Better to serve those on the side.) Do try guava or pawpaw if you have a chance.

1 cup heavy cream, half-and-half, or milk
5 to 7 tablespoons organic sugar or half as much agave nectar
One 3-inch piece vanilla bean, slit lengthwise in half
2 cups cultured low-fat buttermilk or kefir
One 1/4-ounce envelope unflavored gelatin

1. Rub 6 small ramekins or dariole molds with almond oil. Heat the cream with the sugar and the vanilla bean in a small saucepan. Once it reaches a boil, turn off the heat. Pour the buttermilk into a bowl and set it over the cream for 15 minutes to remove the chill. Meanwhile, stir the gelatin into 1/4 cup cold water and let stand for 5 minutes to soften.

2. Remove the buttermilk. Take the vanilla bean out of the cream and scrape the seeds back in, reserving the pods to make vanilla sugar (page 27).

3. Bring the cream to a near boil, then turn off the heat and add the softened gelatin. Stir until it's completely dissolved, then whisk in the buttermilk. Pour the mixture into the ramekins and refrigerate until set, about 3 hours.

4. To serve, dip each ramekin into hot water, run a knife around the edge, and turn it out onto a plate.

swedish creams and panna cotta

BEFORE THE PANNA COTTA CRAZE BEGAN, I used to make Swedish cream, a recipe that came from my pastry assistant at Café Escalera in Santa Fe. Next to anything chocolate, it was the most popular dessert at the restaurant. We set this creamy gelatin-based dessert in narrow pans and served it sliced and adorned with fresh fruits, fruit sauces, chocolate, or sometimes a combination of all three. With its affinity for fruit, chocolate sauce or shavings, and caramel, Swedish cream was hardly ever served the same way twice.

Panna cotta is a similar quivery creamy white dessert. The main difference is the sour cream in the Swedish version and sweet cream in the panna cotta. These desserts are, like the original Swedish cream, based on cultured dairy.

Dariole molds, or timbales, and ramekins that hold a scant $1/2$ cup when filled to the brim are perfect containers for these custards (filled less, though). A drop of almond oil smeared around the interior makes them easy to unmold. I sometimes use French café wineglasses, top them with fruit, and enjoy the creams directly from the glass without unmolding them at all. The richer the dairy, the more stunning the dessert, but if you're using cream and whole-milk yogurt, you might want to make smaller portions. In such cases I use espresso cups and serve the cream with an espresso spoon.

While I love the black flecks that come from using vanilla beans, vanilla in this form can be very costly. Replace it in each version with vanilla extract if you wish.

One of the beauties of Swedish creams, aside from how easy they are to make, is that they can be paired endlessly with fruit, in the form of compotes, finely diced fruit, or vivid fruit sauces, such as those made from cherries, apricots, and berries.

Yogurt-Honey Ice Cream MAKES 1 QUART

THERE'S NO CUSTARD to make here—you just bring three ingredients together and end up with a soft, honey-flavored tangy ice cream that goes with pretty much every fruit dessert in this book. However, it can also be a dessert in itself, served with toasted nuts and warm honey spooned over the top.

The goodness relies on the quality of the yogurt—it should be creamy and smooth with a distinctive flavor. And as for the honey, choose one whose flavor you really enjoy. If you love strong, dark honey, use it here.

The first day the texture of the ice cream will be soft, but by the second day it will be a little chalky because of the small amount of sweetener. Put the frozen yogurt in the refrigerator about 30 minutes before you plan to serve it and the texture will be perfect. Best to use it the first day, though.

1 cup heavy cream
3/4 cup honey, plus extra for serving
3 cups yogurt, preferably organic whole-milk

Warm the cream with the honey in a saucepan, stirring occasionally, until dissolved. There's no need to bring it to a boil. Stir this mixture into the yogurt, then whisk to smooth out the texture. Refrigerate until cool. Freeze in an ice cream maker according to the manufacturer's directions. Then transfer to a container and keep in the freezer until ready to serve. Serve alongside a fruit dessert or with honey, warmed and spooned over each portion.

YOGURT-MAPLE ICE CREAM WITH SHAGBARK HICKORY NUTS

Make the Yogurt-Honey Ice Cream using maple syrup in place of the honey. Taste the mixture to make sure it's sweet enough before freezing and add more maple syrup if need be. Serve with warm maple syrup and toasted hickory nuts.

Swedish Cream with Maple Sugar and Crème Fraîche SERVES 6

THE CRÈME FRAÎCHE, as well as
the hint of butterscotch from the
maple sugar, sets this cream
apart from the others. I think
of this as better suited for
winter, and as such, you might
serve it with the Apple Cider
Syrup (page 252), or small
dried fruits simmered in port
or wine (pages 267 and 269).

2 cups half-and-half or heavy cream
One 3-inch piece vanilla bean, slit lengthwise, or 1 teaspoon
    vanilla extract
6 tablespoons maple sugar
One 1/4-ounce envelope unflavored gelatin
1 cup crème fraîche or sour cream

1. Rub 6 ramekins or dariole molds with almond oil. Heat
the half-and-half with the vanilla bean, if using, and sugar,
slowly bringing it to a boil. Let stand, off the heat, for
15 minutes, then remove the pods and scrape the seeds
into the pan. Set them aside to use in vanilla sugar
(page 27). Stir the gelatin into 1/4 cup cold water and set
aside to soften for 5 minutes.

2. Return the half-and-half to the stove, and with the heat
on low, add the softened gelatin to the pan and stir until it
is completely dissolved. Whisk in the crème fraîche and the
vanilla extract, if using. Pour the mixture into the prepared
molds, glasses, or espresso cups and refrigerate until set,
about 3 hours.

3. To serve, dip each ramekin into hot water, run a knife
around the edge, and turn it out onto a plate. Spoon your
chosen sauce or fruit around each or serve them in their
glasses or espresso cups, unadorned.

Yogurt Swedish Cream SERVES 6

While the word *yogurt* might signal health and virtue, this dessert shouldn't lead you to believe you're dieting. In fact, it's the rich, whole-milk yogurt with the cream on top, plus extra cream, that give this dessert its slinky, silky texture. Try it with a dark velvety sauce made from Blackcap raspberries (page 256) or any of the fruit-based sauces in Chapter 11. Or serve with lightly sweetened berries.

However, not all Swedish creams have to be so rich, and sometimes a lighter dessert has its appeal, too. If that's the case, use low-fat yogurt and low-fat milk in place of the cream. Or compromise by using whole milk (instead of cream) with a reduced-fat yogurt.

1^1/2 cups organic whole-milk yogurt
^{1}/2 cup milk
1 cup heavy cream
4 to 6 tablespoons organic sugar or half as much agave nectar
One ^{1}/4-ounce envelope unflavored gelatin
1 teaspoon vanilla extract

1. Rub 6 small ramekins or dariole molds with almond oil. Combine the yogurt and milk in a bowl. Heat the cream with the sugar in a small saucepan, bringing it just to a boil, then turn off the heat. Set the bowl of yogurt over the pan to take away its chill, giving it a stir once or twice. Meanwhile, sprinkle the gelatin over 1/4 cup cold water and let stand for 5 minutes to soften.

2. After 15 minutes, remove the yogurt, add the vanilla, and reheat the cream. Once the cream is ringed with bubbles, turn off the heat, add the softened gelatin, and stir until it's completely dissolved. Gradually stir the yogurt into the cream-gelatin mixture, then divide it among the ramekins. Refrigerate until set, after 3 to 4 hours.

3. To serve, dip each ramekin into hot water, run a knife around the edge, and turn it out onto a plate. Spoon your chosen sauce or fruit around each or serve unadorned.

Milk and Honey Custard SERVES 6

I WOULDN'T RECOMMEND using chestnut, eucalyptus, or any other extremely strong honey here, but by all means drizzle such honeys over the top if they're favorites. For baking, use something less aggressive—orange blossom, lavender, wildflower—or the deeper Greek thyme honey. Darker honey will burnish the surface of your custard to a coppery hue.

Bake the custard in custard cups or ramekins (you'll need four to six) or a simple earthenware dish. As always, a water bath ensures a smooth texture. Serve with toasted slivered almonds, garden strawberries, or sugared, macerated blackberries.

3 cups milk or 2 cups milk plus 1 cup cream
1/2 cup honey
Pinch of salt
3 eggs plus 1 egg yolk (optional)
1/4 teaspoon freshly grated nutmeg

1. Bring the milk just to a boil with the honey and salt. Lower the heat and simmer for 30 minutes to reduce the milk. Taste and add more honey if you think it's needed. Meanwhile, whisk the eggs, taking care not to create too many bubbles.

2. Preheat the oven to 350°F. Heat water for the water bath. If you are using a single baking dish, be sure that you have a larger dish that it can fit into with ease and still leave room for the water bath.

3. Stir the hot milk into the eggs, then pour the mixture through a strainer into a 4-cup liquid measuring cup. Set the ramekins or dish in the larger baking dish and divide the milk among them. Pour the boiling water into the larger dish to come at least an inch up the sides. Grate or sprinkle a little nutmeg over the top.

4. Bake in the center of the oven until the custards are set except for a small spot in the center, about 45 minutes. Remove from the oven and lift the custards out of the water. Let cool to room temperature. Serve at room temperature or chilled.

Cream Cheese Mousse SERVES 8 OR MORE

I CAN'T THINK of a fruit this wouldn't go with, but for starters, think of serving it with succulent figs, a dollop of a good fruit preserve, or any roasted or sautéed fruit. Requiring no cooking, and keeping well for a week, this mousse is a worthy dessert.

You can put Cream Cheese Mousse together in different ways, using lighter ingredients such as low-fat or full-fat Greek yogurt, ricotta, or cottage cheese.

8 ounces natural cream cheese

1 cup cottage cheese, yogurt, or ricotta cheese

2 tablespoons organic sugar or vanilla sugar (page 27) to taste

One 2-inch piece vanilla bean, slit lengthwise, or $1/2$ teaspoon vanilla extract

$1/2$ cup heavy cream

1. Put the cream cheese and cottage cheese in a food processor with the sugar. Unless you're using vanilla sugar, scrape the seeds of the vanilla bean with a knife into the food processor bowl or add the vanilla extract. Process until the mixture is smooth. Taste for sugar and add more if desired. Add the cream and process until, once again, the mixture is thick and smooth.

2. Line a strainer with dampened cheesecloth and set it over a bowl. Scrape in the mixture, fold the cloth over the top, and press down on the cheese to even it out. Drain for a few hours, refrigerated. It will not yield much liquid—only a teaspoon or so overnight.

3. For serving, the mousse is handsome presented whole, turned out onto a plate lined with fig or grape leaves, but a small portion can be shaped into an attractive oval with two spoons or an ice cream scoop.

Ricotta Mousse SERVES 8 OR MORE

HERE'S AN ORANGE-SCENTED ricotta that you can make and serve immediately, but if time allows, let it drain for the flavors to fuse and to make it more firm. Enjoy it with an exceptional fruit preserve, or have it for breakfast on toast. Chocolate lovers might add broken bits of good chocolate and dust it with cocoa. Prunes Simmered in Red Wine (page 147), Figs in Pedro Ximénez (page 148), or the Nearly Candied Quince (page 89) are fine winter accompaniments while fresh fruit compotes and sauces speak to summer. You might drizzle some Blood Orange Caramel (page 259) over the surface or serve a small scoop with Medjool Dates with Citrus and Walnuts (page 163). Clearly, this mousse is a companion to all kinds of fruits.

You can make this in any quantity. I often make just half or even less if it's just a few of us for dinner.

1 pound (2 cups) ricotta cheese
1/2 cup crème fraîche or heavy cream
5 tablespoons confectioners' sugar
Finely grated zest of 1 lemon or orange
2 tablespoons Essensia Orange Muscat wine or Vin Santo

1. Mix the ricotta with the crème fraîche in a food processor until smooth, then stir in the sugar and citrus zest. It should be a little on the fluffy side rather than dense. If not, add more crème fraîche until it is. Stir in the wine and serve or go on to the next step.

2. Moisten a piece of cheesecloth and line a sieve large enough to hold the ricotta. Turn the ricotta into the cloth, fold the cloth over the top, and place the strainer over a bowl. Refrigerate for several hours or overnight for the flavors to infuse and for any liquid to drain away. (If it's going to drain longer than a few hours, wrap the whole thing in plastic wrap so that the ricotta doesn't pick up odors of other foods.)

3. To serve, open the cloth, turn the cheese onto a plate, and pull the cloth away, leaving its imprint behind. Serve the cheese utterly plain or with vanilla sugar (page 27), preserves, or whatever strikes your fancy.

Ricotta and Goat Cheese Tart in a Nut Crust

MAKES ONE 9-INCH TART, SERVING 8 TO 10

THIS SWEET-SAVORY TART is tangy and a little unexpected. In winter, serve it with glistening dried fruits in wine syrup or a spoonful of fine jam—giving you a cheese, wine, and fruit course in one—but don't ignore summer fruits. Especially good are fresh figs, sugared mulberries, huckleberries, or raspberries.

As for the proportion of goat cheese to ricotta, use twice or even three times as much ricotta as goat cheese, especially if you're not sure about the impact such a singular cheese will make. The goat cheese should be in the fresh, mild style.

THE NUT CRUST

$1/2$ cup walnuts or pecans

$1/4$ cup whole wheat pastry flour

$1/2$ cup all-purpose flour

$1/4$ teaspoon salt

3 tablespoons organic light brown sugar

4 tablespoons ($1/2$ stick) cold unsalted butter, cut into small pieces

1 tablespoon walnut oil or unsalted butter

$1/2$ teaspoon vanilla extract mixed with $1/4$ cup cold water

THE FILLING

8 ounces ricotta or cream cheese (about 1 cup)

4 ounces mild goat cheese (about $1/2$ cup)

$1/4$ cup honey, plus extra for the top

$1/8$ teaspoon salt

$1/2$ cup sour cream or crème fraîche

2 eggs

1. Preheat the oven to 375°F. Put the nuts, flours, salt, and sugar in a food processor and pulse several times to break up the nuts. Add the butter and oil and pulse until crumbly. Add the vanilla water and pulse just until the dough looks moist. When gathered in your hand, the crumbs should adhere. If it seems way too dry, add more cold water, drop by drop. Wipe out the bowl and return it to the food processor.

2. Press the dough into a 9-inch tart pan, evenly building up the sides. Refrigerate briefly until firm, then place on a sheet pan and line with foil and dried beans or pie weights. Bake for 15 minutes, or until the foil comes cleanly away from the crust. Remove the foil and weights, return the tart shell to the oven, and bake 5 minutes more. Reduce the oven temperature to 350°F.

3. Combine the ingredients for the tart filling and puree in the food processor until smooth. Pour the filling into the tart shell and bake until set, 25 to 30 minutes. It may swell but will collapse and become even as it cools. Remove and let cool to room temperature.

4. Serve each slice with a spoonful of fresh or preserved fruit on top or on the side and a drizzle of the fruit's syrup. Or drizzle honey over the surface and serve with fresh fruit.

some cheese and fruit pairings

AMERICAN CHEESE MAKING has become an impressive success, with scores of cheese makers producing fine cheeses—frequently using milk from their own herds of sheep, goats, and cows. Our cheeses now compete in quality with the finest artisanal European cheeses. It's an exciting time for those of us who love cheese and like to buy locally.

In travels around the country I've discovered excellent cheeses at our farmers' markets from Washington State to Wisconsin (of course!) and Vermont (naturally!), but also in Colorado, Indiana, Arizona, North Carolina, and other not-quite-so-obvious places. There are, it turns out, good cheese makers in most every state. Given that these cheeses are, for the most part, handmade in relatively small quantities and sold mostly locally, they can be viewed as regional foods, with distinctive qualities of *terroir* that join them with local fruits, nuts, honey, and preserves. A helpful guide to American cheeses is *The Atlas of American Artisan Cheese* (Chelsea Green Press), by Jeffrey Roberts, who has identified cheese makers by region, as well as their cheeses and where they can be found.

Cheese can be a knife-and-fork or even a spoon food, depending on its texture. With fruit alongside, I like to put out thinly sliced bread, especially a walnut bread or one that's filled with nuts and dried fruits, although a plain baguette is fine, too. You might end up spreading a soft cheese over the bread and then putting some fruit on top, making the most delicious little open-faced sandwich.

As both nuts and fruits have natural affinities for cheeses, aligning cheese, nuts, and fruit from the same areas makes for some distinctive regional cheese plates. Following are just a few of the virtually countless combinations you might consider. As always, it's a good idea to keep our minds as well as eyes open, look at what's regional, and give the unexpected a try. And serve all but the freshest of cheeses at room temperature so that their subtle flavors, lost if they're cold, can be enjoyed.

FRESH SHEEP'S OR COW'S MILK RICOTTA
with Fruit

∾

Although not quite as common as aged cheeses, sheep's and cow's milk ricotta does show up at farmers' markets, and there are some fine handcrafted samples to be found at good cheese shops. The sheep's milk variety is more (pleasantly) pungent than the cow's milk, but both should be light and smooth. I can't imagine a fruit that doesn't go with fresh ricotta cheese—figs (fresh or dried), wine-poached prunes, sautéed plums, roasted pears, and oranges in orange caramel. Sheep's milk ricotta with a slice of succulent summer melon and roasted peppercorns? Yes!

Or take out that special honey you've been saving—chestnut from Italy, the rare Volcano Island honey from Hawaii, or one from your neighbor's backyard. Make a mound of ricotta and drizzle the honey over it. Nothing could be simpler.

CLABBERED COTTAGE CHEESE
with Berries, Golden Apples, or Nearly Candied Quince

∾

This is real cottage cheese from the Cowgirl Creamery in Pt. Reyes, California, a company that makes many distinctive (and award-winning) cheeses that can be found at its Ferry Plaza Market shop in San Francisco, as well as nationally. Cottage cheese with light and creamy curds like this one is a rare find. It's a case of a food we seldom give a second thought coming suddenly and exquisitely into focus. I'd spoon a mound of these soft, milky curds onto a plate and surround them with clusters of mixed berries and golden apples, drizzled with a light honey or the Nearly Candied Quince on page 89. This carefully crafted small-batch cottage cheese makes a surprisingly good dessert—or breakfast.

CREOLE CREAM CHEESE
with Heritage Strawberries

∿

Creole cream cheese is similar to Neufchâtel—maybe a bit tangier—and other fresh, cultured cheeses, but I mention it because of its story: a century and a half ago it was made by French settlers in the New Orleans area; then it disappeared when dairy regulations became too stringent and costly to follow. It remained as a culinary memory until, in very recent years, it was resurrected by Mauthe's Dairy in Louisiana. Once again Creole cream cheese is a New Orleans favorite.

Tangi, one of the small, sweet heritage strawberries from the New Orleans area, would be the perfect fruit to serve here. Just spoon some of the cheese onto a plate, sprinkle a little sugar over it—vanilla sugar (page 27) would be especially nice—and surround with strawberries, sliced and lightly sugared first if necessary. Finally, pour a little cream over the top, as you would for a coeur à la crème.

Both Creole cream cheese and Louisiana heritage strawberries, two of the earliest listings on Slow Food's Ark of Taste, can be found at the Crescent City farmers' market in New Orleans.

FRESH FIGS
with Pure Luck Goat Cheeses and Texas Pecans

∿

Austin's Boggy Creek Farm has the most glorious farm stand where owner-farmers Carol Ann Sayle and Larry Butler, with the help of family and friends, sell their organic vegetables and fruits. They also sell cheeses from Pure Luck goat dairy in nearby Dripping Springs. There's a big fig tree by the back porch and pecan trees on the other side of the house. My idea of an Austin or Texas Hill Country dessert would be to unwrap a log of Pure Luck's Sainte Maure and slice off a piece of its Hopelessly Bleu cheese, put them out with a bowl of ripe figs and another of toasted pecans, and just nibble back and forth among them until they're gone.

PLEASANT RIDGE RESERVE
with Shagbark Hickory Nuts

∾

Tami Lax, chef and owner of Harvest restaurant in Madison, Wisconsin, serves roasted shagbark hickory nuts with Wisconsin farmstead cheeses. Two of her favorites are Pleasant Ridge Reserve, a nutty cow's milk cheese from Uplands Cheese Company, and the aged Bleu Mont Dairy's Bandaged Cheddar, which can be bought at the Dane County farmers' market, across the street from Harvest. (They can also be ordered online; see Resources.)

Put thin slices of the room-temperature cheeses on a plate. Toast the nuts just long enough to bring out their aroma and to color them slightly, then let them cool. Toss them with a pinch of sea salt or leave them plain. Set a little pile of the nuts on the plate with the cheeses.

SOUTH MOUNTAIN DAIRY'S CHEBRIS
with Pecan-Raisin Bread

∾

Cheese makers Marge Peterson and Donna Lockridge, from their dairy farm near Albuquerque, New Mexico, make several farmstead goat cheeses including a tangy fresh chevre, salt-rubbed feta, handsome pyramids with an ash center, crottins, a firm cheese made in the Havarti style, and a soft goat Camembert. However, their runny Brie-style goat cheese, Chebris, which aligns their goats' milk with a traditional recipe, is creamy, a bit tangy as it ages, and divine with a slice of pecan and raisin studded bread from Santa Fe's Sage Bakehouse. Both goat cheeses and fruit- and nut-studded breads seem to show up often where there are cheese makers and bakers—perhaps not the same in each place, but with individual charms intact. Together they make a simple but beguiling dessert.

South Mountain dairy also makes an old-fashioned New Mexican country cheese that they call Queso Lizette—a simple queso blanco that was traditionally sliced and drizzled with honey. The tangy cheese and the sweet, complex honey, eaten with a little bread or some crackers to hold them, are a simple but exciting pair. Include a slice of peach or apple in season and you have dessert.

PIERCE POINT
with Pears

∽

Cheeses, like fruits, can be seasonal, and this complex cheese from Cowgirl Creamery is available only during the fall and winter months, the same months for apples and pears. Cowgirl co-founder Peggy Smith likes it with slices of pear that have been sautéed with honey and lemon thyme, picking up the herb in the cheese. Try the Pears in Honey Caramel on page 86 and add a small snippet of fresh thyme to the caramel.

SPECIAL SELECT DRY JACK CHEESE
with Pears

∽

Vella's Dry Jack cheese from Sonoma, California, is now an American classic. The nearly two-year-old eight-pound wheels are rubbed with a distinctive mixture of oil, cocoa, and pepper, and the cheese is dry and full of flavor. Arrange thin slices on a plate with the Pears in Honey Caramel (page 86) or fresh pears and walnuts. Serve with a light, fizzy Moscato di Asti wine.

NEW YORK CHEDDAR
with Dessert Apples

∽

If I had a wedge of a remarkable Cheddar with some age on it—and I'm thinking of one from the Union Square Market in New York I once bought—I'd set it beside one of the exceptional dessert apples I would hope to find there as well, such as a Cox Orange Pippin, a Golden Russet, or maybe a Pitmaston Pineapple. Or I'd happily have it—and any of our other great domestic Cheddars—with a slice of warm apple pie or on a plate with the Nearly Candied Quince on page 89.

BLUE CHEESES
with Walnuts and Dates

∽

Serve a slice of Maytag Blue or Pure Luck's Hopelessly Bleu—one cow and one goat cheese—with toasted walnuts, fresh figs, and ripe melon in late summer, dates in winter, and a glass of port. At some point you'll have to forgo fresh figs, but dried ones would be an excellent substitute.

SALLY JACKSON'S SHEEP'S MILK CHEESE
with Pears

~

Sally Jackson's cheeses don't wander too far from their northwestern home, but if you can, put one of her elegant chestnut-wrapped sheep's milk cheeses on a plate, serve it with fresh pears, any variety that's perfectly ripe and ready to eat, and toasted hazelnuts.

PT. REYES BLUE
with Honey

~

There are people making blue cheeses in all styles throughout the country, but I'm especially fond of Pt. Reyes Blue, which can be bought more easily than others. It looks delicate but has a strong presence. Try it with honey, some thinly sliced bread, or some lightly toasted walnuts. The honey is slightly startling with the cheese but also just right.

GOAT MILK PAVE
with Blenheim Apricots

~

I found this and two other delectable cheeses from Pug's Leap goat dairy at the Healdsburg farmers' market in California. Although I don't usually think of apricots with cheese, they made a memorable pairing. The Pave, aged only about three weeks, comes in a pyramid shape and is soft, with a white bloomy rind. Have both the cheese and the apricots at room temperature.

PEDROZO'S BLACK BUTTE RESERVE
on Toast

~

The Pedrozo family in Orland, California, produces twenty-pound wheels of cheese from their own grass-fed cows. Their prize-winning Black Butte Reserve is made with spring milk from Jersey cows and aged six months, for release in September. It's a firm, buttery golden cheese with plenty of presence. The family likes it on toast, with a fine jam or fruit. It makes a great dessert grilled cheese sandwich that you can make in a toaster oven.

TELEME
with Dried Fruit Compote

~

Not all great domestic cheeses are new. Teleme cheese, made in California since 1917 and nationally available, is based on the Italian cheese called Stracchino, a delicious, tangy, soft running cheese. Peluso's version is square and dusted with rice flour. At room temperature, Teleme is so soft you can spoon it onto bread. It's creamy yet sprightly with either citrus or mushroom tones, depending on its age. Serve a young Teleme with bread and a spoonful of a dried fruit compote (page 142), the juices reduced to a syrup and spooned around the plate, or one of the quince dishes.

HOSHIGAKI AND FUYU PERSIMMONS
with Roasted Walnuts and
Bandage-Wrapped Cheddar

∾

Hoshigaki are Hachiya persimmons that are hung in the cool autumn air and massaged daily for six weeks until the flesh is dry and covered with the fruit's own sugars. This laborious Japanese process, which is still practiced in California, means hoshigaki are expensive, so you'd never just bite into one for a casual snack. Amelia Saltsman, who finds these at the Santa Monica farmers' market, serves hoshigaki as an appetizer with walnuts, pepper, and cheese. This is also good for dessert—especially with a slice of fresh persimmon. The aged bandage-wrapped Cheddar from Fiscalini Farmstead Cheese Company reflects the salty, nutty, and fruity flavors on the plate.

Slice 1 or 2 hoshigaki into 1/2-inch-wide strips. Peel, then thinly slice 2 Fuyu persimmons. Toast 1/2 teaspoon peppercorns in a dry skillet until aromatic, then crush them lightly with a mortar. Lay the persimmon strips and slices on a plate. Add a small handful of lightly toasted walnuts and thin shavings of Fiscalini's bandage-wrapped Cheddar. Drizzle a few drops of walnut oil over both the persimmon and the cheese and season with pepper and a little fleur de sel.

CHAPTER 10

· Five Cakes to Go with Fruit ·

Here are five cakes with very different personalities and virtues, but they also share two characteristics: none is made with fruit, but they all go with fruit.

Nor do any of these cakes require icings or buttercreams. The light and airy Olive Oil Orange Chiffon Cake, an improved variation of a cake that I've been making for years, is especially lovely with citrus compotes and stone fruits, particularly sliced white nectarines. Another favorite of mine is the Yeasted Sugar Cake, whose plain but faintly yeasty flavor makes it especially attractive with berries, peaches, and pears. The Steamed Chocolate Cake is pure chocolate and light as a feather, and chocolate, as we know, is good with all kinds of fruits, such as sautéed cherries, berries, poached prunes, caramelized plums, and any versions of these prepared in red wine. Fruit sauces, found in the next chapter, also add a welcome sharp fruit bite to a chocolate cake.

The Almond-Corn Flour Cake makes use of almond paste, a rather special ingredient that produces a moist, sturdy cake that is attractive with all stone fruits and drupes, whose seeds, when bitten, taste of almond. For a fast little cake, there's the Brown Sugar-Ginger Cream Cake, a good winter cake to have in one's emergency repertoire. If made with white sugar rather than the moist, dark brown types, it takes on the kind of neutrality that can host a number of toppings, from plain nuts to crushed amaretti, when texture and crunch are desired, whether or not fruit is to be served.

Despite their tendencies to align themselves with particular fruits, these cakes, in fact, can be served confidently with all kinds of fruits. Of course, they can also stand alone, without fruit or cream or anything else to make them complete.

Olive Oil–Orange Chiffon Cake A TALL 10-INCH CAKE, SERVING 10 TO 12

THIS IS AN impressive tall cake with a flavor that's not quite recognizable, provided by the olive oil, which is used in place of the usual bland "salad" oil. While cake flour is highly refined and a far cry from the whole-grain flours we're rightly urged to eat, it does make a cake that's flawlessly light, and this is one of the times I do use it. Use a nonstick angel-food cake pan, rub the sides and bottom with butter, and then dust it with sugar to give the cake a subtle crunch. This cake is lovely served with all kinds of fruits, from sugared strawberries to nectarines to citrus compotes.

2^1/2 cups sifted cake flour
2 teaspoons baking powder
^{1}/2 teaspoon fine salt
6 eggs, at room temperature, separated
^{1}/4 teaspoon cream of tartar
1 cup organic white sugar
1 teaspoon vanilla extract
2 teaspoons orange-flower water
Finely grated zest of 2 large tangerines or oranges
^{1}/2 cup olive oil (one pressed with lemon would be lovely)
Juice squeezed from the orange, plus water to make 1 cup
Confectioners' sugar for dusting

1. Preheat the oven to 350°F. Butter an angel-food cake pan and dust with turbinado or granulated sugar.

2. Sift the cake flour after measuring it and then a second time with the baking powder and salt and set aside.

3. Using the whisk attachment of a standing mixer, beat the egg whites until just foamy, then add the cream of tartar. Whisk until they begin to form peaks and then gradually add ^{1}/3 cup of the sugar and continue whisking until firm peaks are formed. Avoid getting them too stiff; softer whites will fold more easily. Scrape the whites into a large bowl.

4. Using the same mixing bowl (don't bother to rinse it), beat the yolks with the remaining ^{2}/3 cup sugar on high

speed until thick and light colored, 4 to 5 minutes. Lower the speed and add the vanilla, orange-flower water, and zest, then slowly add the oil.

5. Gradually pour in the juice; then sprinkle on the flour by spoonfuls until all is added. Remove the bowl from the mixer stand and reach thoroughly around the bottom of the bowl with a rubber scraper to make sure all the dry ingredients are mixed in.

6. Pour the batter over the egg whites, then fold together using about 8 strokes. Pour the batter into the pan and bake until tall, golden, and pulling away from the pan, 45 to 50 minutes.

7. When done, don't invert the cake; leave it upright to cool. To speed things up, you can lift the cake out of the pan, but leave it attached to its bottom. When cool, use a knife if necessary to separate the cake from the pan, invert it onto a platter, and dust with confectioners' sugar.

Serve with

Citrus with Orange Caramel (page 59)

Fresh Cherry Compote (page 261) and whipped crème fraîche

Blackberries with Rose Water (page 42) or Blackberry Fool (page 206)

Whipped cream and fruit or just fruit between layers of the cake

1 cup cream, softly whipped and sweetened with 1 tablespoon confectioners' sugar, ¼ teaspoon vanilla extract, 1 teaspoon orange-flower water, and the juice of a very dark blood orange to tint it pink

½ cup apricot preserves stirred into whipped cream

Almond–Corn Flour Cake

THIS ALMOND-RICH CAKE, which is made entirely in a food processor, will serve you well. Moist, dense, and tremendously pleasing, it goes with all kinds of fruits—especially dried ones—but can stand proudly alone. I first started making this cake using a portion of Iroquois roasted white corn flour, which gives it a subtle, toasty flavor. So does a handful of finely ground cornmeal, but resist using that coarse, golden polenta—the bits are too large for this cake. Corn flour is a better choice.

Bake in an 8- or 9-inch round pan, a loaf pan, or individual ramekins to make cakelets. For a more rustic presentation, use a Spanish terra cotta dish, one intended for gratins.

3¹/₂ ounces almond paste (¹/₂ package of Odense)
²/₃ cup organic sugar
8 tablespoons (1 stick) unsalted butter, at room temperature
3 eggs, at room temperature
1 teaspoon vanilla extract
¹/₄ teaspoon almond extract
¹/₂ cup sour cream or yogurt
²/₃ cup corn flour
²/₃ cup all-purpose flour
³/₄ teaspoon baking powder
¹/₄ teaspoon salt
Confectioners' sugar for dusting

1. Preheat the oven to 375°F. Butter and flour your baking pan or dish. If using a pan without a removable bottom, line the bottom with a round of parchment paper.

2. Pulse the almond paste with the sugar in a food processor until evenly combined. Add the butter and pulse until well amalgamated. With the machine running, add the eggs one at a time until well blended. Scrape down the sides, then add the flavorings and sour cream and blend until smooth. *(continued)*

3. Mix the flours, baking powder, and salt together in a separate bowl, then add half to the batter and pulse 3 times. Add the second half and pulse 3 times again. Scrape the bowl to make sure everything is well combined, give it 3 or 4 more pulses, and then pour the batter into the prepared pan and even the surface. Bake in the center of the oven until golden and starting to pull away from the pan, about 35 minutes for a 9-inch cake, about 20 minutes for individual cakes.

4. Cool for 10 minutes, then turn the cake onto a serving plate and peel off the paper if you used it. Dust with confectioners' sugar.

Serve with

Figs in Pedro Ximénez (page 148)

Sautéed Plums with Cardamom (page 84)

Small Dried (Dark) Fruit in Port or Pedro Ximénez (page 267) or Small Dried (Light) Fruit in Sherry or Sweet Wine (page 269)

Warm Berry Sauce (page 255)

Yeasted Sugar Cake MAKES ONE 9-INCH ROUND CAKE, SERVING 6 TO 8

ENDOWED WITH EGGS and butter, although less by far than in any conventional cake, this cake possesses a tender crumb and a warm, yeasty fragrance. Its subtle personality makes it a match with any juicy compote—and it can also serve as a fine base for a grand strawberry shortcake.

Despite the presence of yeast, this yields a sticky batter rather than bread dough, so it's easiest made in a mixer using a paddle attachment or by hand, with the aid of a strong arm and a wooden spoon. The only trick is to have your butter very, very soft and the eggs warmed before starting.

$1/4$ cup organic sugar

One $1/4$-ounce envelope active dry yeast

$1/2$ cup warm milk

1 egg plus 2 egg yolks, at room temperature

1 teaspoon vanilla extract

$1/2$ teaspoon salt

2 cups all-purpose flour

5 tablespoons unsalted butter, softened

THE TOPPING

1 tablespoon unsalted butter, melted

1 to 2 tablespoons organic sugar—white, light brown, or a mixture

1. Butter a 9-inch springform, tart, or cake pan. Dust with granulated sugar. Put $1/4$ cup warm water in the bowl of an electric mixer. Stir in 1 teaspoon of the sugar and the yeast. Set aside to proof.

2. In a separate bowl, whisk the warm milk with the egg and yolks, vanilla, remaining sugar, and salt. When the yeast is foamy, with the mixer on low speed, beat in the milk and egg mixture. Start adding the flour $1/2$ cup at a time and beat on medium speed until smooth.

3. Once all the flour has been added and the batter is smooth, scrape down the bowl once or twice to make sure everything is incorporated, then beat in the soft butter. Raise the speed to medium-high and beat until the batter

is smooth and glossy, 2 to 3 minutes. Scrape the batter into the prepared pan and smooth it out.

4. Because the batter will adhere to any covering, I let it rise uncovered. Although a slight skin will develop on the surface, it disappears when baked. Set aside in a warm place for an hour to rise. After an hour, preheat the oven to 350°F. Just before baking, brush the melted butter over the top and sprinkle with the sugar.

5. Bake in the center of the oven until springy yet nearly firm, with the sugar melted into the butter to form a glaze over the top and down the sides, about 40 minutes. Remove from the oven, release the sides of the springform pan right away, and let cool. If using a tart pan, put on kitchen mitts and carefully remove the rim before the sugar sets. Serve warm or at room temperature. Leftovers make great toast the next morning.

Serve with

Late Summer Rhubarb and Blackberry Compote
(page 73) or Baked Rhubarb with Vanilla, Orange, and Clove (page 80)

Strawberries with Maple Sugar and Cream (page 204) or any of the fruit-cream combinations

Strawberries in Red Wine Syrup (page 64)

Blueberry or Huckleberry Compote (page 258)

Brown Sugar–Ginger Cream Cake SERVES 8

I LOVE HOW a cream cake comes together so easily, its tender crumb and its neutral pound-cake-like personality. But until I started playing around with different sugars, it always seemed too bake-shop bland. Like shortbread, the rather neutral ingredients show off whatever sugar (or flour) you use. Maple sugar is subtle and warm, while the superdark organic brown sugar or muscovado make a caramel-like cake that calls out for ginger and a bit of pepper. In the end, it's a great cake for fall and winter, when we turn to apples, pears, and dried fruits.

$3/4$ cup all-purpose flour

$3/4$ cup cake flour

$1^1/2$ teaspoons baking powder

$1/4$ teaspoon salt

2 eggs, at room temperature

1 cup heavy cream

1 cup maple sugar, dark muscovado, or organic dark brown sugar

$1^1/2$ teaspoons ground ginger

$1/8$ teaspoon freshly ground pepper

1 teaspoon vanilla extract

1. Butter and flour a loaf pan or an 8-inch springform pan. If using a loaf pan, line the bottom and ends with parchment paper. Preheat the oven to 350°F.

2. Combine the flours, baking powder, and salt in a large bowl and whisk them together. Make a well in the middle.

3. Using the whisk attachment of an electric mixer, beat the eggs until foamy, then add the cream, sugar, and flavorings. Beat until you have what looks like soft whipped cream. (If using maple sugar, the cream may not thicken, but the cake will still work.) Pour the mixture into the center of the flour mixture and whisk together just until well combined and free of lumps. Scrape the batter into the pan and even it out.

4. Bake until a cake tester comes out clean, 50 to 60 minutes. Let cool for 15 minutes, then remove the rim or turn the cake out of the pan and remove the paper. Cool before slicing.

VARIATIONS

Omit the ginger and pepper for a more straight-ahead brown sugar cake.
Use white sugar and you'll have a cake that will go with virtually all fruits, fresh or in a compote.
Cover the surface of the cake, before baking, with ½ cup crushed amaretti crumbs, pine nuts, slivered almonds, or chopped pecans. Press them lightly into the batter so that they'll stay attached as the cake rises.

Serve with

Plump Golden Apples (page 76)

Pears in Honey Caramel (page 86)

Roasted Mission Figs with Honey (page 88)

Steamed Chocolate Cake SERVES 8 TO 10

STEAMING, RATHER THAN baking, produces a smooth, domed cake that is unfailingly moist and chocolate-dark with a fine, resilient crumb. The top begs to be crowned with whipped cream, candles, holly, or festive flowers, and fruit accompaniments should not be ignored. Here's where you can look to dried fruits, fruits in wine, and any fruits that possess a bit of acid.

To improvise a pudding mold, use a bowl with a two-quart capacity—glass, metal, or crockery—and butter it well. Make sure it will fit in a Dutch oven that has a tight-fitting lid. The bowl needs to rest on something. I use the lid of a canning jar or a tuna fish can with both ends removed. Allow $1\frac{1}{2}$ hours for steaming. The more chocolate you use, the fudgier the cake will be. If you prefer a fine crumb, use the smaller amount.

6 tablespoons unsalted butter, sliced, plus extra for the bowl

4 to 6 ounces dark chocolate, 60% to 70% cacao

2 tablespoons brewed espresso or strong coffee

1 cup organic light brown sugar

4 eggs

$\frac{2}{3}$ cup milk

2 teaspoons vanilla extract

$\frac{1}{2}$ teaspoon almond extract

$1\frac{1}{2}$ cups all-purpose flour

$\frac{1}{2}$ cup unsweetened cocoa powder

$1\frac{1}{2}$ teaspoons ground cinnamon (optional)

2 teaspoons baking powder

$\frac{1}{4}$ teaspoon salt

1. Generously butter a 2-quart glass, metal, or ceramic ovenproof bowl. Melt the butter with the chocolate and espresso in a small skillet over very low heat. Whisk together the sugar, eggs, milk, and extracts in a large bowl.

2. In a smaller bowl, whisk the flour, cocoa, cinnamon if using, baking powder, and salt together. When the chocolate has melted, stir to smooth it out and whisk it into the egg mixture until smooth. Next add the dry ingredients in 3 stages, again whisking until smooth after each addition. You will end up with a smooth, glossy batter. Turn it into the buttered bowl. Cover tightly with a sheet of buttered foil, buttered side down, and then with a second layer of foil.

3. Set the bowl on a canning jar lid or other heatproof support inside a Dutch oven. Pour in hot water to come at least a third of the way up the sides and bring to a boil. Reduce the heat so that the water just barely boils and cook for 1½ hours. Remove the bowl, holding the rim with a towel. Carefully remove the top layer of foil, which will have quite a bit of moisture on it, then remove the second layer. The cake should be firm and pulling away a little from the sides of the bowl and dry when a cake tester is inserted. If it seems too soft in the center, cover again and return to the Dutch oven for another 5 minutes, or until done, then remove the foil.

4. Place a cake plate over the top; grab both bowl and plate and invert. The cake will fall onto the plate. Serve warm or at room temperature with any of the following fruit accompaniments. (If you're taking the cake to a party, simply leave the bowl on it and remove it when you arrive.)

Serve with

Dried Cherries in Red Wine (page 266)

Strawberries in Red Wine Syrup (page 64)

Raspberry Coulis with Muscat Wine (or other berry sauce) (page 260)

Small Dried (Dark) Fruit in Port or Pedro Ximénez (page 267) or Small Dried (Light) Fruit in Sherry or Sweet Wine (page 269)

Apricot Sauce with Cardamom (page 254)

CHAPTER 11

❧

· Sauces Made from Fruit ·

These fruit-based sauces, whether chunky or smooth, are so easy to make that they should hardly count as recipes. Yet I include them because they can become such a useful asset in your kitchen. Their clear colors and pure flavors complete so many simple preparations, from unadorned creams to cakes, puddings, and fruits. In addition, many of these sauces keep well in the refrigerator and the freezer.

Consider these recipes when you have fruit on hand that's ripe and must be used immediately—apricots about to turn to jam on their own, an excess of berries or peaches, that dead-ripe persimmon sitting on the counter—or apple cider or pear juice that might ferment otherwise. Frozen fruit, whether you've frozen your own or bought it, is not out of the question either. I consider frozen black raspberries and wild blueberries a welcome resource, for they make luscious, fruit-dense sauces.

An excess of dried fruits isn't likely to be a problem, of course. All those beautiful dried fruits you gleaned from the market, when cooked in wine, are right in step with winter. After a few days, dried cherries that have been simmered in a red wine syrup yield their pronounced cherry flavor—lovely with ricotta cheese or a cheese tart.

When I'm somewhat at wits' end, I can be assured of a respectable last-minute dessert knowing that I can drizzle a chunky warm blackberry sauce over ice cream, spoon spiced peaches around a Swedish cream, or drizzle warm pear caramel over sautéed pears. There are also fruits that haven't been included here that should be considered. Imagine a sauce made of lychees, for example, or mangoes or kiwis. The possibilities are endless.

❧

Apple Cider Syrup MAKES 1 GENEROUS CUP

IT SOUNDS LIKE quite an extravagance to reduce a quart of apple cider or pear juice to a cup, but it produces an incredibly intense liquid with a subtle taste of caramelized fruit—and with no sugar added. Spoon it over ice cream or around the semolina pudding (page 180), and, of course, with any dessert that features apples or pears. Remember this the next time you have excess apple juice or a windfall of apples. Running them through the juicer will provide you with the best juice.

The addition of crème fraîche smooths out any rough edges of acidity, but those who don't eat dairy can simply leave it out. With the dairy the syrup keeps for weeks in the refrigerator, without it—for months.

1 quart apple or pear cider, preferably organic
1 teaspoon arrowroot or organic cornstarch dissolved in
    1 tablespoon water
1/2 cup crème fraîche, or more if the caramel is very dark

Bring the juice to a boil in a 3-quart saucepan. Lower the heat, then cook at a low boil until a little over a cup remains, after about 45 minutes. Keep a measuring cup nearby, and after about 35 minutes start pouring the juice into it to judge how far you have to go. Toward the end the juice will take on a deep caramel hue.

Version One

For a thin and not so intense sauce, stop at this point and whisk in the diluted arrowroot and crème fraîche.

Version Two

For a more intense caramel, continue reducing the juice until bubbles cover the entire surface and the liquid is quite dark but not burned. (You can tell by the smell.) As soon as it reaches this point, remove it from the heat and immediately add about 1/4 cup water or juice to stop the cooking. Return the pan to the heat and stir to break up the clumps of caramel, then whisk in the crème fraîche.

Apricot Sauce with Cardamom MAKES A SCANT 2 CUPS

Spoon this lush, electric-orange sauce around a Swedish cream or serve it with the Cream Cheese Mousse (page 222). This is easy to multiply and equally easy to divide.

1 pound ripe apricots, halved and pitted
3 to 4 tablespoons organic sugar, agave nectar, or simple syrup
1/2 teaspoon ground cardamom

Put the apricots in a small saucepan with the sugar, 1/2 cup water, and the cardamom. Bring to a boil, then lower the heat, cover the pan, and cook over low heat until the fruit has fallen apart, after about 10 minutes. Set a strainer over a bowl or a glass measuring cup, pour in the fruit, then force the pulp through the strainer with a rubber spatula. Taste the sauce to make sure it's sweet enough—apricots can taste very tart when cooked. If so, add more sweetener to taste.

Warm Berry Sauce MAKES ABOUT 2¹/₂ CUPS

THIS CHUNKY, BERRY-DENSE sauce is one for a bowl of fine ice cream or a rice pudding. Despite the measurements given, this is the kind of dessert topping you can throw together with different kinds of berries, perhaps some remaining from another recipe or the odd handful or two from your garden. Use one or several kinds of berries, especially those related to blackberries, such as olallieberries and marionberries. Nonrelatives, like huckleberries with blueberries, work here as well.

1 tablespoon unsalted butter
3 cups organic mixed berries or a single variety
3 tablespoons maple sugar or organic light brown sugar
2 teaspoons orange-flower water, Kirsch, or Grand Marnier

Melt the butter in a skillet or saucepan over medium heat. Add the berries, sprinkle on the sugar, and cook until the berries have released their juices and softened, after about 2½ minutes. Toss them as they're cooking to distribute the sugar. Remove them from the heat and add any of the flavor additions, starting with 2 teaspoons and then adding more to taste. As they sit, the juices will emerge more fully and intensify. Serve warm or at room temperature.

Blackcap Raspberry Sauce MAKES 1 SCANT CUP

I USE FROZEN berries since I can't get fresh ones. Blackcaps are dark little fruits with a distinct winey flavor. This sauce is so intense that you can use it sparingly. Spoon it over peaches or intensify a berry tart by spooning it over the fruit once it's cooked.

2 cups frozen or fresh Blackcap or black raspberries
2 tablespoons organic sugar
Few drops fresh lemon juice, to taste

Put the berries in a small saucepan over medium heat. Add the sugar and ⅓ cup water. Bring to a boil and cook just to soften the fruit, about 2 minutes, then pour it into a sieve set over a bowl. Force the pulp and the juice through, leaving the seeds behind. Add a few drops of lemon juice, or more to taste, then pour into a clean jar and refrigerate.

Red Currant Sauce   MAKES ABOUT 1 CUP

You CAN FORTIFY this clear carmine sauce with a few drops of cassis or leave it just as it is. It makes a vivid accompaniment to a plain poached peach or pear. And it also makes a pretty and refreshing flavoring for a glass of seltzer. Store in the refrigerator and use over a period of weeks.

1 cup red currants
2 tablespoons agave nectar or $^{1}/_{4}$ cup organic sugar or other sweetener, to taste
Crème de cassis

If you have currants that are on their stems, pluck them off with your fingers or run a fork through the clusters to remove the berries. This will pluck them right off. Put them in a small saucepan over medium-high heat with a few tablespoons of water. Once they start to split, lower the heat, cover the pan, and cook until the fruit is soft, after 5 to 10 minutes. Force the fruit through a sieve, pressing out every drop of juice that you can. Measure it. For 1 cup, you'll probably need 2 tablespoons agave nectar or ¼ cup sugar to sweeten it. If using sugar, heat it with the juice until it dissolves. Add a few drops of cassis and let cool before using.

Blueberry or Huckleberry Compote

MAKES ABOUT 2 CUPS

THESE LITTLE BERRIES are cooked just long enough to warm them through and tease out their juices. Serve warm or cold with the Cream Cheese Mousse (page 222), Ricotta Mousse (page 223), or plain ricotta. Or let the berries cool, then fold them into a sabayon and spoon over peaches.

2 cups huckleberries or blueberries, wild if possible

Grated zest and juice of 1 small lemon or 1 large lime

$\frac{1}{8}$ teaspoon ground cinnamon

$\frac{1}{8}$ teaspoon ground or freshly grated nutmeg

$\frac{1}{4}$ cup maple syrup or maple sugar

2 teaspoons arrowroot or 1 teaspoon cornstarch mixed with 2 tablespoons water

Put the berries in a small saucepan with the lemon zest and juice, cinnamon, nutmeg, and syrup. Add 1 tablespoon water and cook over moderate heat just until the juices run, after 10 minutes or so. Add the dissolved arrowroot and continue cooking for a few minutes longer, until clear.

Blood Orange Caramel MAKES ABOUT $1/2$ CUP

THIS BURNISHED ORANGE caramel benefits from the acidity of the citrus, making it more interesting as well as more attractive than caramelized sugar. The juices that accumulate from, say, sautéing plums or peaches can be used in the same way. This will keep indefinitely in the refrigerator. If stiff, warm in a pan of simmering water to loosen.

$1/3$ cup granulated sugar
$1/2$ cup freshly squeezed blood orange or other citrus juice

Melt the sugar over medium heat in a medium light-colored skillet, stirring often until the sugar turns a rich, but not too dark, caramel color. Standing back from the pan, slowly pour in the juice. It will bubble ferociously, and the caramel will clench into a knot, but don't worry. Cook, while stirring, and after about 5 minutes the caramel will have dissolved.

Raspberry Coulis with **Muscat Wine** MAKES ABOUT 1²/₃ CUPS

THIS CLEAR RED juice can adorn desserts from chocolate cake to baked custards to luscious Swedish creams and poached peaches. And it can also serve as a broth for a raspberry soup (see page 69). Leftovers can be frozen and taken out as needed.

I use frozen, unsweetened organic raspberries because local berries are uncommon where I live and terribly expensive when they are available. Frozen fruits work just fine in a sauce.

3 tablespoons granulated or organic sugar
3 cups frozen unsweetened organic raspberries
3 to 4 tablespoons orange Muscat wine or Beaumes de Venise
1 teaspoon fresh lemon juice, or more to taste
2 teaspoons arrowroot or cornstarch dissolved in
    2 tablespoons water (optional)

1. Bring ²/₃ cup water to a boil in a small saucepan with the sugar, give it a stir, and simmer until the sugar is dissolved. Add the raspberries, simmer for 1 minute, and then turn off the heat and let the fruit stand in the syrup for 5 minutes. Force the juice through a sieve with a pestle or a rubber spatula. Stir in the wine and the lemon juice and let cool.

2. For a sauce with a little more body, add the diluted arrowroot to the juice, simmer while stirring until clear, after a few minutes, cool, and add the flavorings below if desired.

RASPBERRY COULIS WITH SWEET HERBS
Simmer the water and sugar for 3 minutes with 2 sprigs of lavender, 6 lemon verbena leaves, or 2 rose geranium leaves, first crushed in your fingers.

Fresh Cherry Compote MAKES ABOUT 2 CUPS

I USE ABOUT 1 tablespoon sugar for 1 cup pitted cherries, which may leave them a little too tart for some. I'm assuming that the accompanying dessert is sweet, but you can easily add more sugar or maple or agave syrup or stevia, all of which have the advantage of dissolving instantly into the fruit. Three cups or so of sweet cherries is a good amount for six servings, whether they go alongside the Pistachio-Cardamom Torte (page 160), around a Swedish cream, or over ice cream. I've called mostly for sweet ones, since they're usually the ones we have on hand, but a few pie cherries mixed in will boost that cherry flavor.

2$\frac{1}{2}$ cups sweet red cherries, such as Bing, Lambert, or Van
$\frac{1}{2}$ cup or more sour cherries, if available
$\frac{1}{4}$ to $\frac{1}{2}$ cup organic sugar, to taste
2 tablespoons Kirsch or maraschino liqueur

Pit the sweet cherries with a cherry pitter. For the pie cherries, gently squeeze the seed to push it out the stem end into a bowl. When all are pitted, put the cherries in a wide skillet in a single layer. (Do this in 2 batches if needed.) Sprinkle the sugar over the fruit, then turn the heat to high. After a minute, give the pan a shake. The sugar will melt and the cherries will begin to release their juices. After 4 minutes they should be sufficiently soft. Turn off the heat, add the Kirsch, and turn the cherries and the sauce into a bowl. Serve warm or refrigerate and serve cold. As they sit, they'll give off even more juice.

Passion Fruit Sauce MAKES ABOUT ½ CUP

IN TRUTH, PRETTY much all you
have to do is slice passion fruit
in half, scoop out the seeds and
pulp, and spoon it over whatever
you're serving. But should you
find yourself with a number of
ripe fruits and no plans for them,
you can preserve them this way to
use later. Even though wrinkled,
ready-to-eat passion fruits look
remarkably inert, they continue
to dry out and eventually ferment,
which, if you've paid $2 or $3 for
each, is a painful waste to endure.
Better to make a little sauce that
you can use or store for a while.

Four or five fruits don't make
a lot of sauce, but even a few
tablespoons will be a lifesaver
when you need something
special for dessert. This is good
spooned over vanilla ice cream
and especially over pineapple.

4 or 5 passion fruits
2 tablespoons simple syrup

Take each fruit, hold it over a bowl, poke a gash in it with
a knife, and pull the fruit apart so that all the precious
juice goes into the bowl and not on the counter. Then scoop
out the flesh with its seeds. Do this with all the fruits.
Stir in the simple syrup. Refrigerate or transfer to a small
but heavy-duty plastic bag and freeze. Use within a few
months.

Guava or Pineapple Guava Puree MAKES ABOUT 1 CUP

IF YOU DELIGHT in the tropical flavor of guavas and feijoas, or pineapple guavas, and are fortunate enough to have a glut of them that you must use, turn them into a puree. You can spoon it over ice creams or use it as a base for a homemade ice cream or Swedish cream. And either puree would make a tremendous smoothie!

Strawberry guavas are a gorgeous salmon pink, while feijoas are a duller beige. Despite the difference in appearance, the flavor of each is soft and tropical.

1 pound guavas or pineapple guavas
$1/2$ cup organic sugar
One 1-inch piece vanilla bean, slit lengthwise

1. Halve the fruits and scoop out the flesh. Combine ½ cup water and the sugar in a small saucepan, bring it to a boil with the vanilla bean, and simmer until the sugar is dissolved, giving it a stir to help things along. Add the fruit and simmer for 2 minutes, or long enough to soften the fruit, then turn off the heat. Lay a piece of parchment paper directly over the fruit to keep it from darkening.

2. Cool the fruit in the syrup. Scrape the seeds out of the vanilla bean, then work the soft fruit through a sieve to separate the pulp from the skins. Store, covered in the refrigerator, where it will keep for a few weeks, or freeze.

Warm Spiced Peaches to Serve Over Ice Cream

MAKES ABOUT 2 CUPS

SERVE THE FRUIT warm or at room temperature over ice cream. An apple-balsamic vinegar found at the San Francisco Ferry Plaza farmers' market is perfect here, as it combines both fruit and sugar, but an apple *or* balsamic vinegar will be good, too. While the vinegar lifts everything up, it shouldn't be too pronounced— we're talking only a few drops.

4 ripe peaches, preferably freestone
1/4 cup organic sugar
2 cinnamon sticks
4 cloves
5 cardamom pods
Few drops vinegar

1. Dip the peaches into boiling water for 5 to 10 seconds, then immediately transfer them to a bowl of cold water. Peel the peaches, then thickly slice into a 10-inch skillet.

2. With the heat on high, sprinkle the sugar over the fruit and add the spices to the pan. Then lower the heat and cook, turning the fruit gently until a thick syrup emerges, after 15 to 20 minutes.

3. Let cool, then taste. Add a few drops—or more—of vinegar just to sharpen the flavors and bring them more into focus.

PERSIMMON PUREE
makes about 1 cup

∾

IF YOU HAVE ripe persimmons that you just can't get to, you can turn the pulp into a silky bright orange sauce to garnish a winter dessert, such as the date pudding on page 164 or the Native Persimmon Pudding on page 194.

Gently squeeze the pulp of fruit into a sieve, then press it through with a rubber scraper, leaving behind any bits of skin and the occasional seed. Stir in simple syrup to taste and add brandy or Frangelico. Transfer to a container, press a piece of parchment or plastic wrap directly on the surface to keep it from turning brown, and cover with a lid. It will keep for 3 to 5 days in the refrigerator or 6 months in the freezer.

Dried Cherries in Red Wine MAKES 1½ CUPS

I'VE FOUND ALL kinds of dried cherries at farmers' markets, as well as fresh ones—sour pie cherries, Bing, Rainier, and other varieties that you can't always find in groceries. Even dried sour cherries have that distinctive cherry pie flavor that the sweet ones do. I've used both separately and mixed together when I have some of each but not a full cup of one. You might need to add a little more sweetener if you're using all sour cherries.

1 cup dried cherries, sweet, sour, or a mixture
¼ cup organic sugar, or more to taste
1 cup red wine
¼ teaspoon crushed black peppercorns
2 teaspoons arrowroot or cornstarch
1 or 2 drops almond extract

1. Put the cherries, sugar, and all but 2 tablespoons of the wine in a small saucepan and bring to a gentle boil. Add the pepper and stir to dissolve the sugar. Cook over medium heat until the cherries are soft, about 10 minutes.

2. Dissolve the arrowroot in the remaining 2 tablespoons wine. Stir this into the cherries and cook for another minute, or until the sauce is clear and just a little thickened. Turn off the heat and add the almond extract. Store in a clean jar and refrigerate. After a few days, the cherry flavor will begin to emerge. Kept refrigerated; the cherries keep for weeks if not months.

Small Dried (Dark) Fruit

in Port or Pedro Ximénez MAKES 1 CUP

YOU CAN MAKE this in any quantity—I make several cups at a time and keep it to draw from over the winter months—but a cup is an economical and useful amount. In this mixture I use dark fruit with a little color coming from golden raisins and/or dried apricots. Add spices or just let the flavor of the wine and fruit shine through. As the fruit steeps, it will plump. Use it to garnish simple desserts, such as the Ricotta and Goat Cheese Tart (page 224) or a Ricotta Mousse (page 223).

1 cup dried fruit, such as large Red Flame raisins, golden raisins, a few apricots, Black Mission figs, prunes, currants, and cherries
1½ cups port or Pedro Ximénez
¼ cup honey
1 cinnamon stick (optional)
½ teaspoon toasted peppercorns (optional)
2 cloves (optional)

1. Cut the larger fruit into small pieces about the size of the large raisins, then rinse all in warm water.

2. Bring the wine to a boil with the honey and the spices, if using, then turn off the heat. Drain the fruit, put it in a clean jar, and cover with the wine and spices, if using. Stored in the refrigerator, the fruit will keep for months.

Small Dried (Light) Fruit

in Sherry or Sweet Wine MAKES 1¹/₂ CUPS

THIS IS SIMILAR to the preceding recipe, except that all the fruit is golden, green, and yellow and plumped up in sherry or a sweet Muscat wine. Spoon the fruit over a rice pudding, a wine-poached pear, or the Milk and Honey Custard (page 221). Measurements need not be exact, nor does the mixture. I've made this with just raisins and diced apricots and been happy.

1¹/₂ cups mixed dried fruit, such as green Hunza raisins, golden raisins, apricots, and dried pears
2 cups sherry or Muscat wine
¹/₂ cup organic sugar or ¹/₃ cup honey
Lemon zest removed in broad strips

Cut the fruit into small pieces and cover with hot water. Let it soak while you bring the wine and sugar to a boil in a saucepan with the citrus zest. When the sugar is dissolved, drain the fruit, then add to the syrup. Reduce the heat and simmer, partially covered, until the fruit is tender and the sauce is syrupy, about 30 minutes. Transfer to a clean jar with a tight-fitting lid. Store in the refrigerator for up to 2 months.

SUGGESTED READING (AND VIEWING)

These are some books, both old and new (and one film), that I've found inspiring and helpful.

The Anatomy of Dessert, Edward A. Bunyard, Modern Library Food, 2006

The Atlas of American Cheese, Jeffrey Roberts, Chelsea Green Press, 2007

Chez Panisse Desserts, Lindsey Shere, Random House, 1985

Cornucopia II: A Source Book of Edible Plants, Stephen Facciola, Kampong Publications, 1998

In the Sweet Kitchen, Regan Daley, Artisan, 2001

Melons for the Passionate Grower, Amy Goldman, Artisan, 2002

The Oxford Companion to Food, Alan Davidson, Oxford University Press, 1999

Uncommon Fruits Worthy of Attention: A Gardener's Guide, Lee Rech, Addison Wesley, 1991

Eat at Bill's: Life in the Monterey Market, a film by Lisa Brenneis, www.tangerineman.com/eab.htm

RESOURCES

Most all of the fruits, nuts, and grains referred to in these pages can be found at various farmers' markets across the country, and in some cases it's possible to contact a producer directly. Sources for foods that are on Slow Food's Ark of Taste can be found by going to slowfoodusa.org/ark or to localharvest.org/ark-product.

CHEESES

Black Butte Reserve: Pedrozo Dairy and Cheese Company, realfarmsteadcheese.com

Bleu Mont Dairy bandaged cheddar: cheeseforager.com/bleumont

Clabbered cottage cheese, Pierce Point: Cowgirl Creamery, cowgirlcreamery.com/cheeses

Creole cream cheese: Mauthe's Dairy, mauthes-dairy@aol.com, and slowfoodusa.org/ark

Goat milk pave: Pug's Leap, pugsleap.com

Pleasant Ridge Reserve: uplandcheese.com

Ste. Maure and Hopelessly Bleu: Pure Luck Goat Cheese, purelucktexas.com

OILS AND NUTS

La Nogalera walnut oil: lanogalerawalnutoil.com

Missouri Northern Pecan Growers: mopecans.com

Native pecans: Dohmann Pecan Farms, ortech-engr.com/pecans/farm.html

Shagbark hickory nuts and black walnuts: Ray's Hickory Nuts, rayshickorynuts.com

FRUITS

Bronx grapes and pawpaws: Lagier Ranches, lagierranches.com

Crane melons: cranemelon.com

Heirloom plums and other stone fruits: Andy Mariani, andysorchard.com

Pawpaws: heritagefoodsusa.com and Integration Acres (for fresh, frozen, and canned products), integrationacres.com. Also see the Pawpaw Foundation, devoted to the advancement of *Asimina triloba*, North America's largest native edible fruit: pawpaw.kyhsu.edu.

Pixie tangerines: Ojai Pixie Growers, ojaipixies.com

Wild persimmon pulp: persimmonpudding.com. This Web site, maintained by Barry Nichols, is dedicated to "the growing, education, and use of *Diospyros virginiana L.*, the common or American persimmon." He cannot promise that those listed are willing to ship persimmon pulp, but says that it's worth it to ask.

DATES

Certified organic dates: Flying Disc Ranch, flyingdiscranch.com

Japanese dried persimmons (Hoshigaki): Otow Orchard, otoworchard.com, and slowfoodusa.org/ark

Luscious Medjools: Pato's Dream Date Gardens, oasisdategardens.com, and localharvest.org:80/farms/M6367

Organic Medjools, Deglet Noors, and other varieties: Oasis Date Gardens, oasisdategardens.com

HERBS, SPICES, FLAVORINGS, AND COCOA

Penzeys Spices: penzeys.com

HONEY AND SUGAR

Cane sugar (jaggery): Heavenly Organics, heavenlyorganics.com

Maple sugar, in 1-pound bags: Vermont Country Store, vermontcountrystore.com

Rare Kiawe Hawaiian honey: Volcano Island Honey, volcanoislandhoney.com

GRAIN

Iroquois or Tuscarora cornmeal: slowfoodusa.org/ark and localharvest.org/ark-product

Native wild rice: nativeharvest.com

Organic brown rice: massaorganics.com

Red quinoa: squinoa.net

INDEX

and frangipane galette, Marianne's, 132

hazelnut-stuffed, 78

and raspberries, with honey sabayon, 211

with spirits, 55

warm spiced peaches, 264

white: aromatic fruit plate of melons, raspberries, Bronx grapes, and, 42; in lemon verbena and lavender syrup, 68; red berry soup with summer berries and, 69–71

Pear(s). *See also* Dried fruit(s)

cheese pairings, 86, 230, 231

cream tart with, 139

dried: small dried fruit in sherry or sweet wine, 269

hazelnut-stuffed, 78

in honey caramel, 86–87

poached in red wine with pepper and star anise, 61

ripe pear with toasted five-spice pecans, 52

with spirits, 55

upside-down cake, yeasted, 104–5

Pecan(s), 154

five-spice, ripe pear with, 52

fresh figs with goat cheeses and, 228

minced dried fruit and spice tart, 156–57

ricotta and goat cheese tart in a nut crust, 224–25

sweet and savory, butterscotch pudding with, 188–89

torte, with blackberry preserves, 158–59

walnut-pecan maple tart, 150

Pecan-raisin bread, South Mountain Dairy's Chebris with, 229

Pedro Ximénez

figs in, 148

small dried fruit in, 267

Pepper and star anise, Seckel pears poached in red wine with, 61

Peppercorns, toasted, muskmelon with sea salt and, 48

Persimmons, 50, 195

Fuyu, with Asian pears, figs, and walnuts, 50

late summer fruits with dry-farmed almonds, 45

native persimmon pudding, 194

persimmon fool, 208

persimmon puree, 265

with roasted walnuts and Cheddar, 233

with sea salt, hazelnuts, and hazelnut oil, 50

Pies, 12, 23, 31, 111

apples for, 97

apricot, fold-over, 112

cheese with, 116, 118

Concord grape, fold-over, 116–17

pastry for, 30–31

Pineapple

and kiwi, with basil syrup, 65

with passion fruit, 51

with spirits, 55

Pineapple guava(s), 51

puree, 263

Pine nuts, figs with mascarpone and, 41

Pistachios

chocolate bark with cardamom, sea salt, apricots, and, 169

green, fresh dates and, with goat cheese and fleur de sel, 54

pistachio-cardamom torte with warm cherry compote, 160–61

pomegranate gelée with saffron-yogurt cream and, 202

white chocolate and coconut bark with lavender and tangerine zest, 170

Plum(s), 82–83, 146. *See also* Prune(s)

baked in wine, with orange, sugar, and clove, 81; with rosemary, 81

and nectarine upside-down cake, 106–7

roasted, with Muscat sabayon, 81

sautéed, with cardamom, 84

with spirits, 55

and walnut tart, 113

Poached fruit. *See* Cooked fruit; Dried fruit(s); Fruit in syrup

Pomegranate

gelée, with saffron-yogurt cream and pistachios

seeds, winter jewel compote with, 60

Pomegranate molasses, grapefruit with, 45

Pomelos, 60. *See also* Citrus fruit; Grapefruit

Port. *See also* Wine

melons with, 46

Preserves, 141

blackberry, nut torte with, 158–59

jam and almond tart or bar, 151

three-layer almond tart with, 133

Prune(s), 146. *See also* Dried fruit(s)

prune, quince, and dried cherry compote, 145

simmered in red wine with honey and spice, 147

small dried fruit in port or Pedro Ximénez, 267

Pudding(s), 176–91. *See also* Rice pudding

butterscotch, with sweet and savory pecans, 188–89

dark chocolate, 186

date, not-quite-so-sticky, 164–65

Indian pudding, 176

native persimmon, 194

quinoa, with dried cherries and cranberries, 177

semolina, honeyed, with wine syrup, 180–81

sweet potato-coconut, with toasted coconut, 185

tangelo-tangerine, 190

Puree

guava or pineapple guava, 263

persimmon, 265

rhubarb: green, with grapefruit, 79; red, with maple, cinnamon, and orange, 79; rhubarb fool, 209; rhubarb tarts in a corn flour crust, 124–26

Swedish cream with fruit puree, 214

Quince, 75

braised in honey and wine, 90

nearly candied, 89; with cottage cheese, 227

prune, quince, and dried cherry compote, 145

Quinoa pudding with dried cherries and cranberries, 177

Raisin-pecan bread, South Mountain Dairy's Chebris with, 229

Raisins, 12. *See also* Dried fruit(s)